O LOVE
THAT WILL NOT
LET ME GO

OTHER CROSSWAY BOOKS BY NANCY GUTHRIE

Come, Thou Long-Expected Jesus
Experiencing the Peace and Promise of Christmas

Jesus, Keep Me Near the Cross
Experiencing the Passion and Power of Easter

Be Still, My Soul
Embracing God's Purpose and Provision in Suffering
(25 Classic and Contemporary Readings on the Problem of Pain)

O LOVE
THAT WILL NOT
LET ME GO

Facing Death with
Courageous Confidence in God

EDITED BY
NANCY GUTHRIE

WHEATON, ILLINOIS

Cover design: Amy Bristow

Cover photo: Terry Bidgood, Trevillion Images

Printed in the United States of America

Scripture quotations marked AT are the author's translation.

Where indicated, Scripture quotations are from the ESV® Bible (*The Holy Bible, English Standard Version®*), copyright © 2001 by Crossway. Used by permission. All rights reserved.

Where indicated, Scripture quotations are from the King James Version of the Bible.

Where indicated, Scripture quotations are from *The New American Standard Bible®*. Copyright © The Lockman Foundation 1960, 1962, 1963, 1968, 1971, 1972, 1973, 1975, 1977, 1995. Used by permission.

Where indicated, Scripture quotations are from *The Holy Bible: New International Version®*. Copyright © 1973, 1978, 1984 Biblica. Used by permission of Zondervan. All rights reserved. The "NIV" and "New International Version" trademarks are registered in the United States Patent and Trademark Office by Biblica. Use of either trademark requires the permission of Biblica.

Where indicated, Scripture quotations are from *The New King James Version®*. Copyright © 1982, Thomas Nelson, Inc. Used by permission.

Where indicated, Scripture quotations are from *The Revised Standard Version*. Copyright © 1946, 1952, 1971, 1973 by the Division of Christian Education of the National Council of the Churches of Christ in the U.S.A.

All emphases in Scripture quotations have been added by the authors.

ISBN 13: 978-1-4335-1618-4
ISBN 10: 1-4335-1618-7

Library of Congress Cataloging-in-Publication Data

   O love that will not let me go : facing death with courageous confidence in God / edited by Nancy Guthrie.
     p. cm.
   Includes index.
   ISBN 978-1-4335-1618-4 (tpb)
    1. Death—Religious aspects—Christianity. I. Guthrie, Nancy. II. Title.
BT825.O2   2011
236'.1—dc22   2010023929

Crossway is a publishing ministry of Good News Publishers.

CH   26   25   24   23   22   21   20   19   18   17   16

I fondly dedicate this book to my sister in Christ, Marion Williams Kelley (1929–2009). I had the privilege of sharing the first few chapters of this book with Marion in her final days on this earth. Her joy in these truths, her determination to die well, and her courageous confidence in God's promises, were a living demonstration of the aim of this book, and an inspiration to me as I worked on it.

I am not afraid to look the king of terrors in the face,
For I know I shall be drawn, not driven,
out of the world.

Until then let me continually glow and burn out for thee,
And when the last great change shall come,
let me awake in thy likeness.

THE VALLEY OF VISION

Contents

Preface

I remember when it hit me. I had been pregnant with my son, Matt, for what seemed like forever. There was so much I actually enjoyed about being pregnant, and so much I looked forward to in having a son. But one day the reality dawned on me that to have that son, I was going to have to give birth. I remember thinking that no one simply stays pregnant forever, putting off the inevitable, and I had little control as to when that time would come. I looked at my growing belly and thought, "This baby is going to have to come out one way or another," and it scared me. Pregnancy—good. Baby—good. The process of labor and delivery—I was not so sure.

We sometimes have a similar thought process about death. Life—good. Life after death with God—good. It's that process of labor and delivery into the next life we're not so sure about. In fact, we'd really rather not talk about it or even think about it. Yet I'm convinced that there is a real freedom, and even joy, in thinking it through, and that exploring death in light of the Scriptures can actually soothe our fears and infuse our thoughts about death with hope and peace.

But I also realize that some people might think reading a whole book on the topic of facing death would be a real bummer. Some may think it a bit morbid. And some people, though they might be loathe to admit it, are a bit superstitious about discussing death—afraid that if they have a conversation about it, or give consideration to it, that it might somehow come a little sooner.

There are others for whom death is so relegated to the realm of the fall, that there is no place in their thinking or theology for exploring what it means to face death in a way that pleases and honors God. They have given little or no thought about what it means to anticipate and prepare for death in a way that evidences a solid, God-glorifying confidence in his goodness, his sovereignty, and his promises.

That is what the brief chapters in this book will help us to do. They will help us to turn away from the pervasive denial about death in our culture, and to face squarely the reality of death through the more beautiful and ultimate reality of Christ. It is Christ, and only Christ, who makes facing death bearable. Christ infuses the most painful and perplexing aspects of the end of this life with hope and peace.

I don't mean to imply or suggest that death for the believer is always sweet rapture. In spite of its universal nature, it's still not natural; and it never will be. God has not promised his children an easy death or deathbed visions of glory (although sometimes he is good to give them). He does, however, promise his presence with us. He will be our Shepherd as we walk through the valley of the shadow of death. And he will be waiting to welcome us on the other side.

I recognize that there may be some awkwardness in giving this book or receiving this book from someone else. You need to know that if someone has given this book to you, it's not necessarily that they expect "the worst." You should, instead, assume they want to stand beside you, and open their arms with you, to welcome "the best"— whenever that should come. Solomon wrote, the day you die is better than the day you are born (Eccles. 7:1). Paul described departing this life to be with Christ as "better by far." If someone gave this book to you, they want to believe this with you. Giving this book to someone you care about does not say, "I think you are going to die soon." It says, "Since we are all going to die soon, let's live now like we believe the gospel is true."

Joseph Bayly once wrote, "Christians claim to believe that heaven—being present with God—is so wonderful, and yet act as if going there were the greatest tragedy."[1] The problem is with our perspective, which is so oriented to life here and now. But I believe that taking in and chewing on the truths expressed in this collection of writing by great preachers and theologians of the past and present can radically change how we think and feel about the unavoidable reality of death. Death, for the believer, is no tragedy. And for the believer to die well—to live and die aiming to glorify God, confident that God will make good on all of his promises—this is a thing of great beauty.

I invite you to join me in pursuit of a life and death that befits our belief in the gospel. May the truths in this book equip and embolden us to live and die well to the glory of God.

Nancy Guthrie

Part One

A REALITY THAT WILL NOT BE DENIED

1

Only When You Know How to Die Can You Know How to Live

J. I. PACKER

In today's world, death is the great unmentionable, just as physical sex was a hundred years ago. Apart from cynical paradings of a sense of life's triviality (the Grateful Dead, "he who dies with the most toys wins") and egoistic expressions of belief in reincarnation (the New Age, Shirley MacLaine), death is not ordinarily spoken of outside of medical circles. To invite discussion of it, even in the church, is felt to be bad form.

It has become conventional to think as if we are all going to live in this world forever and to view every case of bereavement as a reason for doubting the goodness of God. We must all know deep down that this is ridiculous, but we do it all the same. And in doing it, we part company with the Bible, with historic Christianity, and with a basic principle of right living, namely, that only when you know how to die can you know how to live.

There is a great contrast here between past and present. In every century until our own, Christians saw this life as preparation for eternity. Medievals, Puritans, and later evangelicals thought and wrote much about the art of dying well, and they urged that all of life should be seen as preparation for leaving it behind. This was not otiose morbidity, but realistic wisdom, since death really is the one certain fact of life. Acting the ostrich with regard to it is folly to the highest degree.

Why has modern Protestantism so largely lost its grip on this biblical otherworldliness? Several factors have combined to produce the effect.

First, death is no longer our constant companion. Until the twentieth century most children died before they were ten, and adults died at home with the family around them. But nowadays deaths in the family are rarer and, as often as not, happen in hospitals, so that we can easily forget the certainty of our own death for years together.

Second, modern materialism, with its corollary that this life is the only life for enjoying anything, has infected Christian minds, producing the feeling that it is a cosmic outrage for anyone to have to leave this world before he or she has tasted all that it has to offer.

Third, Marxist mockery of the Christian hope ("Pie in the sky when you die") and the accusation that having a hope of heaven destroys one's zeal for ending evil on earth have given Christians a false conscience that inhibits them about being heavenly minded.

Dying well is one of the good works to which
Christians are called. *Packer*

Fourth, modern Christians are rightly troubled at the cultural barrenness, social unconcern, and seemingly shrunken humanity that have sometimes accompanied professed longings for heaven. We have come to suspect that such longings are escapist and unhealthy.

Fifth, man's natural sense of being made for an eternal destiny, the awareness formerly expressed by the phrase "the greatness of the soul," has largely atrophied amid the hectic artificialities of Western urban life.

How then should Christians think about death—their own death, to start with?

1. Physical death is the outward sign of that eternal separation from God that is the Creator's judgment on sin. That separation will only become deeper and more painful through the milestone event of dying, unless saving grace intervenes. Unconverted people do well, therefore, to fear death. It is in truth fearsome.

2. For Christians, death's sting is withdrawn. Grace has intervened, and now their death day becomes an appointment with their Savior, who will be there to take them to the rest prepared for them. Though they will be temporarily bodiless, which is not really good, they will be closer to Christ than ever before, "which is better by far" (Phil. 1:23).

3. Since believers do not know when Christ will come for them, readiness to leave this world at any time is vital Christian wisdom. Each day should find us like children looking forward to their holidays, who get packed up and ready to go a long time in advance.

4. The formula for readiness is: "Live each day as if thy last" (Thomas Ken). In other words, "Keep short accounts with God." I once heard Fred Mitchell, Overseas Missionary Fellowship director, enforce this thought shortly before his own instantaneous home-calling when the plane in which he was traveling disintegrated in midair. Mitchell lived what he taught, and his biography was justly

given as its title the last message radioed by the pilot of the doomed aircraft—*Climbing on Track*. I hope I never forget his words.

5. Dying well is one of the good works to which Christians are called, and Christ will enable us who serve him to die well, however gruesome the physical process itself. And dying thus, in Christ, through Christ, and with Christ, will be a spiritual blossoming. As being born into the temporal world was our initial birthday, and as being born into God's spiritual kingdom was our second birthday, being born through physical death into the eternal world will be our third birthday.

 Dag Hammarskjöld was thinking Christianly when he wrote that no philosophy that cannot make sense of death can make sense of life either. No one's living will be right until these truths about death are anchored in his or her heart.

Adapted from *God's Plans for You* © 2001 J. I. Packer, published by Crossway.

James Innell Packer serves as the Board of Governors' Professor of Theology at Regent College in Vancouver, British Columbia.

Scripture quotations are from *The Holy Bible: New International Version.*®

2

Death's Sting Is Removed but Its Bite Remains

MICHAEL S. HORTON

Unlike the old churchyards through which one passed on the way to Sunday services, our churches today are likely to avoid contact with the tragic side of life. We call death "passing away"; we change the name "graveyard" to "cemetery," with euphemistic names (Forest Home) that also sound, eerily enough, like the names of the convalescent hospitals they were in before they "passed."

Often, before we can really feel the force and pain of sin and death, we are told to be happy and look on the bright side. One church-growth guru cheerfully announces that we have gone from having funerals to memorial services to "celebrations," not realizing that this is a fatal index of our inability to face the music, whether we're talking about the tragedy of sin itself or the suffering, death, and ultimate condemnation that it brings in its wake.

We aren't morbid when we take sin, suffering, and death seriously as Christians. Rather, we can face these tough realities head-on because we know that they have been decisively confronted by our Captain. They have not lost their power to harm, but they have lost their power to destroy us. This biblical piety is not morbid because it doesn't end at the cross, but it also doesn't avoid it. It goes through the cross to the resurrection. This is why the Christian gospel alone is capable of refuting both denial and despair. The hope of the gospel gives us the freedom to expose the wound of our human condition because it provides the cure. We see this in John's remarkable retelling of the story of Lazarus's resurrection.

Lazarus, along with his sisters, was a close friend of Jesus. Jesus was entreated to come to his ill friend's side when Mary identified him to Jesus as "he whom you love" (John 11:3). The assumption here is that Jesus and Lazarus are so close that all Jesus needed was an announcement of his condition. Surely Jesus would come running.

Their plea for Jesus was not wrong, but short-sighted in its motivation. They were appealing to him for the healing of Lazarus, while Jesus anticipates using his friend's death as an opportunity to signify his person and work. In terms of the unfolding plot, Lazarus is a character in Jesus' story, not vice versa. The glorification of the Son as the Messiah is the real "show" here, as was the case with all of the miracles. They are signs, not ends in themselves.

After a four-day interval between Lazarus's death and Jesus' arrival in Bethany, Martha displays the sort of frustration that one would not have expected a woman of her day to show toward a man in public, much less a rabbi. Yet after scolding Jesus for his tardiness—"Lord, if you had been here, my brother would not have died," she immediately adds, "But even now I know that whatever you ask from God, God will give you" (John 11:21–22). Martha's faith in Jesus is unfailing. He can still turn things around—even after her brother's entombment—"Even now . . . " (John 11:22). It is important to see how here Martha reflects that combination of heart-wrenching disappointment and faith that we find in the Psalms. She does not believe that even death has the last say in the presence of Jesus.

Jesus replies, "Your brother will rise again" (John 11:23). "Do you believe this?" (John 11:26). Jesus presses her to commit herself not just to the theological question of resurrection of the dead, but to him as the Resurrection and the Life! He not only can give life; he is Life.

Jesus is not simply asking Martha to confess that Lazarus will live, but that those who trust in Jesus Christ—even though they die, will be raised to never die again. It's no longer about Lazarus per se. Lazarus's resurrection will be a sign-proof, in fact, of that reality to be inaugurated with Christ's own resurrection from the dead. Even though people will still die despite the arrival of Messiah, they will not remain dead forever but will be raised in the likeness not of Lazarus' mortal body, still tending toward death, but in the likeness of Christ's glorified body.

We recall that many centuries earlier, in the midst of his agony, Job cried out, "I know that my Redeemer lives and that in this flesh I shall behold God" (Job 19:25 AT). And on the witness stand Martha, racked with myriad thoughts and feelings of desperation and hope, brought Job's exclamation up-to-date: "She said to him, 'Yes, Lord; I believe that you are the Christ, the Son of God, who is coming into the world'" (John 11:27). That is the big event in Bethany this day. Without discounting the resurrection of Lazarus still to come in the story, we cannot forget that, as with all of Jesus' miracles, the most amazing thing is the reality that the sign merely announces and the confession that it draws from our lips. This is the faith that perseveres through the countervening evidence of his experience. And it is Martha's as well.

Mary, who had been sitting in the house, joins Martha at this point (vv. 28–32). Perhaps even more despondent than Martha, both at her brother's death and her beloved Master's apparent failure either to care enough or to be powerful enough, Mary, the one who had lavished Jesus' feet with her expensive perfume, has to be called out to the scene by her sister ("The Teacher has come and is calling for you"). Furthermore, upon meeting Jesus she reiterates the charge, "Lord, if you had been here, my brother would not have died" (John 11:32). Mary is not to be blamed here, but to be respected for having brought her doubts as well as her faith to the Savior. Living in denial of tragedy, too many Christians live schizophrenic spiritual lives: outwardly smiling and brimming with trust and joy, but inwardly filled with doubts and anger. They often do not know where to turn, but Mary, like Job and the psalmist, says, "To God, of course." Bring him your doubts, frustration, and even anger. He can handle it. Remember the cross and God-forsakenness of the Beloved: God, too, knows how to sing the blues.

Jesus' own soul now begins to be drawn into turmoil as he sees the mourners and recognizes the wake that death leaves. Suddenly, he finds himself one of the mourners. Here he is not simply a miracle worker who walks on the sea and calms the storms, but a man who is suddenly overtaken by troubled emotions. His own love for Lazarus and his hatred for death overwhelmed him even though he knew what he was about to do. Already emotionally unhinged by Mary's weeping at his feet, Jesus came to the tomb, and we read those two words that deserve their own verse: "Jesus wept" (John 11:35).

Jesus here overthrows the various pagan conceptions of life and death that are as prevalent in our day: stoicism and sentimentalism. Famous for the stiff upper lip, the ancient Stoics believed that the best souls were those who were completely free of emotion. Sentimentalism, as I'm using the term here, refers especially to the romantic philosophers, poets, artists, and theologians who emphasized the heart rather than the intellect as the proper seat of human dignity. Far from resisting emotional expression, sentimentalism celebrates it. While the Stoic realizes that to abandon negative emotions one must banish all emotions, the sentimentalist believes in admitting only the good emotions, always looking on the bright side of life.

"Then Jesus, deeply moved again, came to the tomb" (John 11:38). Look at Jesus' face, hear his scream here. "Deeply moved" hardly captures the emotion of the original language: *enebrimesato*, meaning to snort like a horse in anger; "troubled," *etaraxen*, meaning agitated, confused, disorganized, fearful, surprised, as when Herod was troubled by the wise men (Matt. 2:3); or when the disciples were troubled and cried out in fear when Jesus walked on the sea (Matt. 14:27). Now it is Jesus who is thrown off his horse, as it were. The Lord of Life, he by whom and for whom "all things were created, in heaven and on earth, visible and invisible, whether thrones or dominions or rulers or authorities" (Col. 1:16), now found himself overtaken by grief. More than grief, in fact—anger. And why not? There he stood face to face with "the last enemy" he would defeat in his crusade against Satan. And he "wept."

The marvel in this scene is that Jesus responds thus even though he knows that he will shortly raise Lazarus from the dead. One would expect his countenance to reveal a knowing grin that invites the crowd to anticipate his miracle, but all it shows is anguish. How much more are we allowed to weep when such an interval exists between the death of loved ones and the final resurrection! Theologically, it is the appropriate response to death—not simply because of our own sense of loss or our mourning for the survivors who are dear to us, but because of the loss to the beloved who has died. We do not grieve as others do who have no hope (1 Thess. 4:13), but we do grieve. Death is not a benign passageway to happiness, but a horrible enemy attempting to keep us in the grave. Death's sting has been removed, but its bite remains. It does not have the last word for believers, but it remains the believer's antagonist until the resurrection of the body. The good news is never that one has died, but that death has been ultimately conquered by the Lord of Life.

At the graveside, neither optimism nor pessimism; sentimentalism nor stoicism, tell us what is happening here. Only Jesus' cross and resurrection define the event for us.

Martha trusted Jesus when she moved the stone at his command. Perhaps she had even heard and recalled Jesus' promise, that the hour is coming in which all who are in the graves will hear his voice and come forth (John 5:28). Jesus' own resurrection will be the firstfruits of those who sleep (1 Cor. 15:20), but this resurrection of Lazarus is in a sense the prelude to that great inauguration of the last day. This is the climactic sign because the last enemy is death (1 Cor. 15:26).

The good news in all of this is that the last enemy is death. This means that Jesus accomplished everything in his mission on earth for our complete redemption and glorification. "The sting of death is sin, and the power of sin is the law." That is the bad news. "But thanks be to God, who gives us the victory through our Lord Jesus Christ" (1 Cor. 15:56, 57). Triumph at last outruns, outspends, outstrips tragedy. But it does so at a painful cost.

Triumph at last outruns, outspends, outstrips tragedy.
But it does so at a painful cost.

Death is not a portal to life. Death is not a benign friend, but a dreaded foe. It is not a natural part of life, but the most unnatural part of life you could imagine. But in his death and resurrection, Jesus crushed the Serpent's head, vanquishing the "last enemy" of every believer. This last enemy will one day be overcome for believers in the final resurrection of the dead, but that is because it has already objectively been vanquished in the resurrection of our Living Head. Look at him and see what the whole harvest will be like in the end! In Christ, the end has already begun. The Head will not live without his body. The shape of the future is already present.

Lazarus was raised, but he died. His body thus raised for a time, continued where it left off in its surrender to decay and death. One day, mourners would gather again at Lazarus's tomb, but this time with no expectation of resurrection until the last day. And yet, precisely because of that confidence, precisely because Lazarus's next funeral occurred this side of Easter, they would not mourn that day as those with no hope. After all, word would have reached them by then—perhaps some of them had even been witnesses—of the greater resurrection of Jesus himself, which would take a stand against death on its own territory, so that those united to him by faith will not remain dead. Their bodies will be raised to worship in God's renewed sanctuary.

Death is still an enemy, not a friend; but it is "the last enemy," and it is already defeated so that now death is not God's judgment upon us for our sin but the temporal effects of our participation in Adam's guilt. And because the guilt and judgment are removed, we can both cry out with our Lord in troubled anger at death and yet also sing with the Apostle, "Where O death is your sting? Where O hell is your victory?" (1 Cor. 15:54–55 AT). What we need again is a church that can sing the blue note in a way that faces the real world honestly and truthfully, recognizing the tragic aspect of life as even more tragic than any nihilist could imagine, while knowing that the One who raised Lazarus is now raised to the right hand of his Father, until all enemies—including death—lie in the rubble beneath his feet.

This article originally appeared in the Jan./Feb, vol. 14, no. 1, 2005 edition of *Modern Reformation* and is reprinted with permission. For more information about *Modern Reformation*, visit www.modernreformation.org or call (800) 890-7556. All rights reserved.

Michael S. Horton is the J. Gresham Machen Professor of Apologetics and Systematic Theology at Westminster Seminary California, host of *The White Horse Inn* national radio broadcast, and editor-in-chief of *Modern Reformation* magazine.

Unless other wise indicated, Scripture quotations are from the ESV® Bible (*The Holy Bible, English Standard Version*®).

Scripture quotations marked AT are the authors translation.

3

He Called Death Sweet Names

JOHN PIPER

Andrew Rivet was a Frenchman who was born in 1573 and spent most of his life in Holland as professor of theology at the University of Leyden. He was a great theologian and full of the Holy Spirit and faith, as Luke says of Stephen (Acts 6:5). On Christmas Day 1650, when he was seventy-seven years old, he preached a sermon, and was immediately afterwards taken ill with a severe disease of the abdomen. He died on January 7, 1651.

He had been a devout man of God and a productive scholar for the kingdom for over fifty years. But when he came to die, God—in a very real sense—did more for him in those last few days of life than in all the years before. Listen to what he said just before he died:

> The sense of divine favor increases in me every moment. My pains are tolerable, and my joys inestimable. I am no more vexed with earthly cares. I remember when any new book came out, how earnestly I have longed after it—but now all that is but dust. You are my all, O Lord; my good is to approach to you. O what a library I have in God, in whom are all the treasures of wisdom and knowledge! You are the teacher of spirits—I have learned more divinity in these ten days that you have come to visit me, than I did in fifty years before. [1]

The hour of death became the servant of the saint—his teacher, his sanctifier, the kindler of his worship.

I remember the death of Zeke Rudolf. He was in my wife, Noël's, class at Wheaton one year behind me. He was 5' 10" and 165 pounds—but he had multiple sclerosis. His father was my faculty adviser, Erwin Rudolf. Zeke died in August 1969, three months after graduation. The thing I remember most vividly from what Dr. Rudolf wrote about Zeke's dying was this sentence: Near the end he called death sweet names. Sweet names! Death became a servant with sweet names.

Now let's be very clear about a biblical truth: Death is an enemy. It is not romantic or glamorous or heroic. Death is an enemy! "[Christ] must reign until he has put all his enemies under his feet. The last enemy to be destroyed is death" (1 Cor. 15:25–26 ESV). We were not created by God to die. Death is a curse and an enemy that came into the world through sin (Rom. 5:12).

But while we are avoiding any simplistic, naïve, romantic images of death, let us believe with all our hearts and all our minds and all our might the great truth of our Christian faith:

> "Death is swallowed up in victory." "O death, where is your victory? O death, where is your sting?" The sting of death is sin, and the power of sin is the law. But thanks be to God, who gives us the victory through our Lord Jesus Christ. (1 Cor. 15:54–57 ESV)

And not only the victory, but more than victory:

> Who shall separate us from the love of Christ? Shall tribulation, or distress, or persecution, or famine, or nakedness, or peril, or sword? . . . [No!] In all these things we are more than conquerors through Him who loved us. For I am persuaded that neither death nor life . . . shall be able to separate us from the love of God which is in Christ Jesus our Lord. (Rom. 8:35–39 NKJV)

We are more than conquerors over death through Christ. God gives us the victory over death. But more than victory. Death is defeated by Jesus. He is bound in the chains of resurrection power so that he cannot destroy us. But more than that. More than that! Death is handed over, bound and defeated, as a servant to the church. We are more than conquerors because death is not just defeated and kept from destroying us; it is enslaved and made the servant of God's people.

This is the meaning of 1 Corinthians 3:21–23, "Let no one boast in men. For all things are yours, whether Paul or Apollos or Cephas or the world or life or death or the present or the future—all are yours, and you are Christ's, and Christ is God's" (ESV). Death is yours the way you are Christ's. And you are Christ's to serve him and glorify him. So death is your servant. The enemy is defeated, bound, enslaved, and delivered into the service of the saints.

So it was not naïve romanticizing when Zeke Rudolf "called death sweet names." It was not immature glamorizing or embellishing of death when Andrew Rivet said that he had learned more truth about God during ten days in the valley of death than in fifty years of study. Defeated death had become their servant. The terrible enemy had become the tutor of heaven. So it is with the enemies of God. Even in their destruction they are made to serve the saints. (See 2 Corinthians 12:7 and 1 Corinthians 5:5 where Satan himself is made the servant of the saints of God!)

I want us to see this and be encouraged by it in the case of Stephen—the first martyr of the Christian church. Stephen died a very horrible death, by stoning. But even here death became Stephen's servant—in at least three ways.

Stephen had just preached a message to the Jewish leaders, and his main point was that the essence of their religion was self-worship, not God-worship. They rejoiced in the work of their own hands, not in God (Acts 7:41, 48). When Stephen came to the end of his message, the council was enraged and ground their teeth at him (Acts 7:54).

God's response to Stephen at this moment was exactly the opposite. He filled Stephen with his Holy Spirit (Acts 7:55). This is not exceptional. You can expect God to do this for you if you walk with him. "Though I walk through the valley of the shadow of death, I will fear no evil: for thou art with me" (Ps. 23:4 KJV). God draws near to the dying saint.

First Peter 4:14 says that when you suffer with Christ "the Spirit of glory and of God rests upon you." There is a special grace given to dying Christians. We often wonder, Could I endure suffering for Christ in the hour of persecution—or even in the hour of "ordinary" death? The answer is no, I couldn't, not in myself. But we will not be left to ourselves. There will be extraordinary grace for the extraordinary trial of death. The Spirit of glory and of God will rest upon us.

And when God comes in the hour of our death, he makes the enemy, death, into the servant of his saints.

Notice how it happened with Stephen. First, as the enemy death draws near and opens its jaws to consume Stephen, the Holy Spirit in Stephen turns the jaws of death into a window of heaven. And instead of seeing the stomach of hell and the face of Satan, Stephen sees the glory of God, and Jesus alive standing at the right hand of God. Acts 7:55: "But [Stephen], full of the Holy Spirit, gazed into heaven and saw the glory of God, and Jesus standing at the right hand of God" (ESV).

Do you see how death is stripped of its power here and made the servant of God's servant? It raises its ugly head and threatens to take away from us all the pleasures of bright spring mornings and buds on the trees and warmth on the skin and the colors of fall and the stars in the night sky, but instead it opens the window of heaven and reveals the glory of God. It threatens to take away our most precious relationships, but instead it shows Jesus standing to receive us.

I don't mean that every believer will get the same vision of glory

30

and of Jesus that Stephen got. But I do mean that this is the way the Holy Spirit comforts us when we are dying and robs death of its power. One way or another *he makes death a window to the glory of God* and to Jesus. And for those who love Jesus more than anyone and long for the glory of God more than anything, the sting of death is gone and the power of death is broken. And whether you are a seventy-seven-year-old theologian or a twenty-two-year-old college graduate, you can call death sweet names.

That's the first way that the Holy Spirit makes death serve Stephen: he makes death a window onto the glory of God and the person of Jesus.

The Holy Spirit . . . makes death a window onto the glory of God and the person of Jesus.

Second, the Spirit enables Stephen to see through death a place of fellowship in the presence of Jesus. Acts 7:59: "And as they were stoning Stephen, he called out, 'Lord Jesus, receive my spirit.'"

In other words, not only did the Holy Spirit turn the hour of death into a revelation of the glory of God and of Jesus, he also showed Stephen that the reason Jesus was standing, and not sitting (as it says in Acts 7:55), was to welcome his servant home. So death serves the dying saint not only as a window to see glory, but also as a doorway to enter glory—not only a window to see Jesus, but also a doorway to join him.

The triumph of the saint over death is the calm and confident prayer, "Jesus, receive my spirit." It is as though you are dying in a small cabin in the woods. The door is death and you are moving toward it inch by inch. As it opens, there is a huge, ravenous wolf with bared fangs and furious eyes. At first you are terrified. But then the Holy Spirit opens your eyes, and behind the wolf you see Jesus shining like the sun. He is standing with his arm extended to you and his face smiling. And hanging tight in his other hand there is a brass chain that leads to an iron collar on the wolf's neck. You hesitate for a moment. But then the Spirit gives you strength, and as you put your foot in the threshold and the mouth of the wolf opens, Jesus flings him with a mighty jerk clear out of sight, and you enter into the presence of the Lord of glory. That's the second way the Spirit makes death serve the saint. It's not only a window to see Jesus; it's a doorway to be with him forever.

Finally, the Spirit makes death serve Stephen by drawing out of him the beauty of Christ-likeness in the hour of trial. Acts 7:60: "And falling to his knees cried out with a loud voice, 'Lord, do not hold this sin against them.'"

When Jesus was dying he had said, "Father forgive them, for they know not what they do" (Luke 23:34 AT). Death had failed utterly as a curse to destroy the love and holiness of Jesus. And now, because Stephen was filled with the Spirit of Jesus, death fails again.

The Devil designs for your death to produce despair and hopelessness and self-pity and resentment and bitterness. But the design of the Holy Spirit is very, very different. He destroys the power of death and makes death into an occasion for showing the beauty of Christ. "Lord, do not hold this sin against them." A great triumph of Christlike mercy!

There is a connection between these three ways that the Holy Spirit (Acts 7:55) transforms death from adversary into servant. And this connection shows that the way to die in the power of the Holy Spirit is also the way to live in the power of the Holy Spirit.

When the Holy Spirit opens your eyes to behold and to love the glory of God, and you see and know that Jesus is alive and triumphant at God's right hand, and when the Spirit gives you the will to say, "Jesus, there is no place I would rather be than with you; receive me," then the beauty and the power of Jesus will enter your life, and hopelessness and self-pity and resentment and bitterness will be consumed by the presence of Christ and by the hope of glory.

This is the way we die by the power of the Spirit. And this is the way we live by the Spirit: loving the revelation of God's glory; knowing the triumph of Jesus over all our enemies; trusting ourselves into his welcoming fellowship; and overflowing with his grace to enemies. This is why we seek the fullness of God's Spirit. This is why we are crying out, "Lord, show us your glory."

"O death, where is your victory?" "O death, where is your sting?" The sting of death is sin. And the power of sin is the law. But thanks be to God who gives us the victory through Jesus Christ our Lord. Amen.

Adapted from "The Death of a Spirit-Filled Man," a sermon by John Piper given at Bethlehem Baptist Church, April 21, 1991. This sermon can be found in its entirety at http://www.desiringgod.org/ResourceLibrary/Sermons/ByDate/1991/754_The_Death_of_a_SpiritFilled_Man/.

John Piper is pastor for preaching at Bethlehem Baptist Church in Minneapolis, Minnesota.

Scripture quotations marked AT are the author's translation.

Scripture quotations marked ESV are from the ESV® Bible (*The Holy Bible, English Standard Version*®).

Scripture quotations marked KJV are from the *King James Version* of the Bible.

Scripture quotations marked NKJV are from *The New King James Version* of the Bible.

4

Not of the World

MARTYN LLOYD-JONES

The more I try to live this Christian life, and the more I read the New Testament, the more convinced I am that the trouble with most of us is that we have never truly realized what it is to be a Christian. If only we understood what the Christian really is and the position in which he is placed, if only we realized the privilege and the possibilities of that position, and, above everything, the glorious destiny of everyone who is truly a Christian, then our entire outlook would be completely changed.

In the long history of the Christian church, thinking of every revival and period of reformation, and the martyrs and confessors, there is only explanation: those people knew what it was to be a Christian. They could defy tyrants without any fear; they could look into the face of death and say, "It is well." They knew who they were, and where they were going. They were not afraid of men, of death, or even of hell, because they knew their position in the Lord Jesus Christ, and the result was that these people triumphed.

We must, therefore, consider what our Lord has to say about the Christian. In John 17:6, Jesus says, "I have manifested thy name unto the men which thou gavest me out of the world." The Christian is not of this world, and does not belong to it. In this one section in John 17, Jesus repeats that four times. Verse 6: "I have manifested thy name unto the men which thou gavest me *out of the world.*" Verse 9: "I pray for them: I pray not for the world, but for them which thou hast given me"; again, verse 14: "I have given them thy word; and the world hath hated them, because they are not of the world, even as I am not of the world."

There are only two groups of people in the world today—those who are of the world and those who belong to Christ. In the last analysis there is no other division or distinction that has the slightest importance or relevance. When we all come to die does it make the slightest difference which political party we belong to? Does it matter whether we are rich or poor, learned or otherwise? Does it matter what our social status is? It is all utterly irrelevant; it does not matter. As the old English proverb says, "Death is the grand leveler."

How foolish we are, how superficial we are, to bother ourselves, as we do, with these other distinctions. In light of this, it is vital that we should ask ourselves the question: Am I of the world or am I not? There is only one fundamental distinction and that is whether we belong to the world or to Christ. That is the only thing that matters on your death-bed, the other things will not be of the slightest value to us; they will be utterly insignificant.

> Whether we belong to the world
> or to Christ . . . that is the only thing
> that matters on your death-bed.

To be of the world can be summed up like this—it is life, thought of and lived, apart from God. In other words, what decides definitely and specifically whether you and I are of the world is not so much what we may do in particular as it is our fundamental

attitude. It is an attitude toward everything, toward God, toward *of*
ourselves, and toward life in this world. In the last analysis, to be of *The World*
the world is to view all these things apart from God.

So let us get rid of the idea that worldliness just means going to
the theatre or the cinema; do not think that if you do this or that
you are therefore a worldly person. It is not that, for there are many
people who never do any of these things, but who, according to the
Scripture, are thoroughly worldly-minded. Indeed—and this is a
terrible thing—you can even subscribe to the Christian faith in an
orthodox manner and still be of the world. If anybody disputes this,
let me give you my authority at once. The word uttered by our Lord
to those people who at the last day shall say, "Lord, Lord, haven't we
done this, that, and the other in your name?" is: "Depart from me,
I never knew you—you do not belong, you never have belonged to
me" (Matt. 25:31–46).

There is a hatred of the thought of death in the world today.
People hate it because they are living entirely for this life and for this
world, and they are not prepared to consider anything beyond it.
That is characteristic of the worldly outlook.

It is a terrible thing to think that there are many people around
us who are living this sort of life. Many ordinary, respectable people
are just living life for themselves and their own little family circle.
They never think of God and they never praise him.

The Christian is not like that. The Christian life is centered on *of Christ*
God. His relationship to God is the controlling thing in his life. He's
not perfect, but the basis of his life is centered on God.

This means, therefore, that my governing thought is that I am a
pilgrim and a stranger in this world, going on to God, so I spend my
time in thinking of my soul and of my destiny. I do not get annoyed
when somebody faces me with the fact of death, because I remind
myself of it day by day; I realize that this is the one thing I have to

start with and that I am a fool if I do not. The Christian always holds that his whole life is lived under God and he realizes the nature of life in this world. He is controlling his life so that he does not foolishly spend most of his time and energy in trying to forget that it must come to an end. He deliberately keeps that before him.

Let me put it as strongly as I can. When a man is like Christ, he hates the world—the outlook, not the people—the mentality, the type of life. He realizes it is subtle, in that it is trying to keep him from God, whatever form it may take. He realizes too, that these things are damnable, and against God. They take a pride in something that belongs to a fallen world, and he hates it as Christ hated it. He turns his back upon it, so he prays a great deal to be delivered from it. He separates himself as much as he can to mediate upon heavenly things and he lives his life in the fear of God. "The world passeth away, and the lust thereof but he that doeth the will of God abideth for ever" (1 John 2:17).

Adapted from *The Assurance of Our Salvation* by Martyn Lloyd-Jones, © 2000 by Bethan Lloyd-Jones, published by Crossway.

David Martyn Lloyd-Jones (1899–1981) was minister of Westminster Chapel in London for thirty years.

Scripture references are from the *King James Version* of the Bible.

5

Is Christ Our Sickness–Bearer?

B. B. WARFIELD

When speaking of our Lord's abounding miracles of healing, Matthew says that he did them "that it might be fulfilled which was spoken by Isaiah the prophet, saying, Himself took our infirmities, and bare our diseases" (Matt. 8:17).

Some suggest this means that we have Christ set before us as the sickness-bearer as well as the sin-bearer of his people; that Christ endured vicariously our diseases as well as our iniquities. Some teach that just as there is now no condemnation to them in Christ Jesus, so there can now be no disease to them that are in Christ Jesus.

This error does not lie in the supposition that redemption is for the body as well as the soul, and that the saved man shall be renewed in the one as well as in the other. This is true. Nor does it lie in the supposition that provision is made in the atonement for the relief of men from disease and suffering, which are fruits of sin. This, too, is true. It lies in confusing redemption itself, which is objective and takes place outside of us, with its subjective effects, which take place in us, and in failing to recognize that these subjective effects of redemption are wrought in us gradually and in a definite order.

Ideally, all of Christ's children were saved before the foundation of the world, when they were set upon by God's love, and given by the Father to the Son to be saved by him. Objectively, they were saved when Christ died for them on the tree, purchasing them to himself by his own precious blood. This salvation was made their personal possession in principle when they were regenerated by the Holy Spirit, purchased for them by the death of Christ on their behalf. It was made over to them judicially on their believing in Christ, in the power of the Holy Ghost thus given to them. But it is completed in them in its full effects only when at the judgment day they stand, sanctified souls, clothed in glorified bodies, before the throne of God, meet for the inheritance of the saints in light.

Here, you perceive, is a process. Even after we have believed in Christ, and have a title as justified men to the benefits bought for us by his blood and righteousness, entrance into the actual enjoyment of these several benefits remains a process, and a long process, to be completed in a definite order. This is true of the spiritual blessings which come to us through the atonement of Christ. We are no longer under the curse of sin. But we remain sinners. The struggle against indwelling sin, and therefore indwelling sin to struggle against, continues through life. We have not yet obtained, and we are not yet made perfect.

It is little that we continue also physically weak, liable to disease, and certain to die. For the removal of these physical evils, too, provision is made in the atonement. But the benefit here, too, is not received all at once. For us, as in the broader sphere of the world's salvation, death is the last enemy to be conquered. Though we are redeemed by the Lord and no longer under the dominion of sin, the results of sin remain with us.

Inwardly we are corrupt; outwardly we are the prey of weakness and disease and death. We shall not escape from either in this life. Who is there that sins not? And who is there that does not suffer and die? But ultimately we are relieved from both—of indwelling corruption when our sanctification is completed and, having been made holy, we depart to be with the Lord, the Holy One, and of outward weaknesses, at that redemption of the body which, while here below, we only, groaning and travailing in pain, wait for in its due season, that is, at the resurrection, when death shall be swallowed up in victory.

This is the teaching of the Bible; and this is what Christ illustrated when he healed the sick in his ministry on earth that men might see, as in an object-lesson—that provision was made in his substitutionary work for the relief of every human ill. There is included in this, however, no promise that this relief is to be realized in its completeness all at once, or in this earthly life. Our Lord never permitted it for a moment to be imagined that the salvation he brought was fundamentally for this life. His was emphatically an other-world religion. He constantly pointed to the beyond, and bade men find their true home, to set their hopes, and to place their aspirations, there.

Our Lord never permitted it . . . to be imagined that the salvation he brought was fundamentally for this life.

But, we are asked, are there not to be prelibations here? Is there no "intermediate work of healing and recovery for the body" here as there is "a vast intermediate work of cleansing and renewal effected for the soul"[1]? Assuredly. The good man will not fail to be the better for his goodness even in his bodily life. But the Lord, in placing his people in this complex of forces whose regular working constitutes what we call the laws of nature, subjects them, of course, to these laws. We cannot expect to be emancipated from the laws which govern the action of the forces in the midst of which our life is cast. That would be to take us out of the world. No matter how holy we are we must expect, if we cast ourselves from a tenth-storey window, to fall with the same certainty and with the same rate of accelerating velocity as other men. The law of gravity is not suspended in its action on us by our moral character. We cannot grow rich by simply rubbing some Aladdin's lamp and commanding supernatural assistance; economic law will govern the acquisition of wealth in our case as in that of others. When typhoid germs find lodgment in a body, even though it be the body of a saint, they will, under favorable conditions, grow and produce all their dreadful effects with the same certainty with which the seeds of corn which you cast into the ground grow and bring forth their harvest. The same laws on which you depend for the harvest of corn, you may equally depend on for the harvests of disease which you reap year after year.

We live then in a complex of forces out of which we cannot escape, so long as we are in this world, and these forces make for disease and death. We are all left here sick. And if we insist upon being relieved of this sickness, we can expect only the answer which was given to Paul: "My grace is sufficient for thee." (2 Cor. 12:9).

But we do not found here solely on a law of nature. Even the laws of nature are under the control of God in their operation, and we point to the good providence of our God. The Lord is rich in mercy to them that trust in him, and it would be strange indeed if there were no visible and tangible fruits of his mercy perceptible in our bodily life. There is a promise for this life as well as for that which is to come, and it is definitely said that those who seek first the kingdom of God and his righteousness, all these things shall be added.

Are not the providence and grace of God enough for us in this, "our little journey in the world"? Or, dissatisfied with these, are we to demand that the laws of nature be suspended in our case; that, though in the world, we shall, in this sense, too, be not of it?

What scriptural ground is there for expecting miraculous healings of the body through these ages of our earthly pilgrimage, in addition to that benefit which the body obtains from its animation by a renewed and sanctifying soul, from our Lord's watchfulness over it as his purchased possession, from the indwelling in it of the Holy Spirit as his temple, from the Father's listening to the prayers of his saints for its keeping and healing, and from all God's goodness to it in fulfillment of his Word that godliness has the promise of the life that now is as well as that which is to come?

None has been pointed to, and we are constrained to believe none exists. For soul and body we are in the Lord's loving keeping. We trust in him, and he keeps us. There is no specific promise that he will keep us otherwise than by his providence and grace. Do not these suffice for all our needs?

Excerpted from *Counterfeit Miracles* by Benjamin B. Warfield, © 1918 by Charles Scribner's Sons, New York.

Benjamin Breckinridge Warfield (1851–1921) was the principal of Princeton Seminary from 1887 to 1921.

Unless otherwise indicated, all Scripture references are from the *King James Version* of the Bible.

6

Our Faith Is in God, Not in Healing

JOSEPH BAYLY

Most Christians believe that God has power to intervene in any illness, bringing healing. The miracles of Jesus Christ are examples of such intervention up to and including death, the funeral procession, and the grave itself.

Saint James advised the sick to seek healing, and prescribed the means: "Is any among you sick? Let him call for the elders of the church, and let them pray over him, anointing him with oil in the name of the Lord; and the prayer of faith will save the sick man, and the Lord will raise him up; and if he has committed sins, he will be forgiven. Therefore confess your sins to one another, and pray for one another, that you may be healed" (James 5:14–16).

The healing movements of recent years within most denominations and other groups find their basic authority in this New Testament passage. But is the promise absolute, committing God to heal every sickness for which his intervention is sought in conformity with the terms of this passage?

Yes, say some, adding that lack of faith is the only obstacle that can block God's healing activity. And so, when prayer for healing is made, complete conviction that God has healed must follow. The burden of conviction is usually placed on the sick person, although others may bear it for him. Any doubt is banished from the mind, usually by the use of Bible passages related to prayer's efficacy and God's power.

Others believe that the promise of healing is not absolute, but conditional. The condition is God's sovereign will. Every request of man to God, they say, must have the essential element of Jesus Christ's prayer in Gethsemane, expressed or implied: "My Father, if it be possible, let this cup pass from me; nevertheless, not as I will, but as thou wilt" (Matt. 26:39). According to those who hold the first-mentioned view, this sort of praying is self-defeating, since it implies doubt. For doubt is the enemy of faith.

But Jesus responded positively to at least one request for healing that involved an honest admission of doubt. "All things are possible to him who believes," he said to a man who had brought his boy for healing. "I believe; help my unbelief!" the father replied. And Jesus healed the boy (Mark 9:23–24).

The Christian person who learns that he has a limited life expectancy is usually open to the suggestion that he pray for healing or submit to the praying and ministrations of others. What are the effects of prayer for healing on a terminally ill person? Tranquility usually follows, because God has been trusted to do what medical science admittedly is powerless to do. One important element of this sense of peace is usually a fresh experience of God's forgiveness and loving acceptance.

If close relatives of the ill person share his Christian convictions, a sense of God's control, love, and oversight permeates family relationships. A hopeful attitude replaces the black curtain of despair that fell when the medical sentence was pronounced. This "peace of God, which passes all understanding" (Phil. 4:7) usually continues even though the person's condition may progressively deteriorate.

What happens if the prayer for healing is based on belief that

God's promise to heal is unconditional, that lack of faith alone can circumvent healing?

If healing is not immediate or dramatic, depression may overtake the sick person. Normal discouragement over the physical condition may be heightened by a new dimension of self-blame and guilt for not having enough faith. Rarely does the sick person blame the "healer" or friends who are "standing with him" for healing.

He may decide that it is necessary to declare that he is healed, in spite of no evidence, or even of evidence to the contrary. If he is hesitant about committing himself in this way, friends may apply pressure, arguing that such a "stand" is necessary for God to heal.

This declaration of healing leads to unreality and death-denial in which husband or wife must share, or appear to share, along with other members of the family. All relationships of the ill person are strained to a certain extent by this announcement of healing, relations with friends as well as with family.

The attitude of New Testament Christians
toward impending death was acceptance,
not prayer for deliverence.

As a result, life's final months are turned into playacting instead of a mature, deepening experience with God and loved ones, based on a recognition of the possibility (if God does not heal) of separation by death. Heaven recedes as a symbol of hope, and the man of faith looks to continuation of life on earth as the zenith of his desire no less than does the man of no faith. Death becomes faith's defeat instead of heaven's door. *if you believe the above*

In the New Testament, healing was immediate. (When Jesus

cured the blind man of Bethsaida, his miracle was in two stages, but healing was still accomplished on the same occasion that the request was made.) Neither Jesus nor the apostles kept people hanging in order to prove their faith. Nor did they ask them to make a verbal acknowledgment of healing in the face of no evidence, or contrary evidence, as a sign of faith.

The attitude of New Testament Christians toward impending death was acceptance, not prayer for deliverance. In the days before his execution by Herod, John the Baptist sent disciples to Jesus to certify that he was the Messiah, not to plead for God's intervention in John's release and stay of execution.

Saint Paul declared his ambivalence over death or the continuation of life in his letter to Christians at Philippi: "It is my eager expectation and hope that I shall not be at all ashamed, but that with full courage now as always Christ will be honored in my body, whether by life or by death. For me to live is Christ, and to die is gain. If it is to be life in the flesh, that means fruitful labor for me. Yet which I shall choose I cannot tell. I am hard pressed between the two. My desire is to depart and be with Christ, for that is far better. But to remain in the flesh is more necessary on your account" (Phil. 1:20–24).

On a later occasion, faced with imminent death, Saint Paul wrote to a godly young pastor, Timothy. In the letter he did not ask Timothy to pray that he would live rather than be executed—"I am now ready to be offered, and the time of my departure is at hand," was his reassuring word (2 Tim. 4:6 KJV). But he did ask Timothy to bring his cloak, because winter was approaching, and books to read in the prison.

When Stephen was stoned, he did not pray, "Lord, keep me from dying so that I may continue to serve you." His prayer was

Stephen

rather, "Lord Jesus, receive my spirit" (Acts 7:59). And kneeling down, he died.

These illustrations are all related to the imminent termination of life by violent means, through martyrdom. It may be objected by some that they do not apply to ordinary sickness and death. Yet if Satan attempts to thwart a ministry and shorten a life through sickness, his power and work are at least equally as evident in martyrdom. Attitudes then become comparable.

I do not mean to imply that prayer for prolonged life is wrong when a situation appears to be terminal. No indication of this sort is given in the words of Saint James, quoted earlier in this chapter; the opposite seems to be true.

But if such praying obscures the reality of heaven and its joyful prospect for the person who is ill, making it appear that only in prolongation of life on earth may satisfaction be found, it is less than Christian.

A pattern for communicating conviction about divine healing and deliverance from death may be found in the Old Testament account of what Shadrach, Meshach, and Abednego said when King Nebuchadnezzar sentenced them to be executed. "Our God whom we serve is able to deliver us from the burning fiery furnace; and he will deliver us out of your hand, O king. But if not, be it known to you, O king, that we will not serve your gods" (Dan. 3:17–18).

"But if not . . ." Here is an admission that we are fallible, that we may be wrong in our conviction that God will heal and thereby postpone death. (Death is always merely postponed, even if—as for King Hezekiah, when he "turned his face to the wall, and prayed," —for fifteen years [2 Kings 20:2].)

What we declare in these words is that our faith is in God, not in healing. Whether we live or die does not affect our bedrock faith in Jesus Christ. And death, not healing, is the great deliverance from all pain and suffering. Death delivers God's people from the hands of persecuting governments, from the ravages of disease, and from every evil affliction.

A friend of mine who died recently had prayed for God to heal him. He was convinced that God had answered and healed; but after a brief remission, the illness returned with full, terrible force. This could have been a devastating blow. But his final months, after surgery and chemotherapy, were not lived under any cloud. Instead he was quietly confident, radiant with Christian hope.

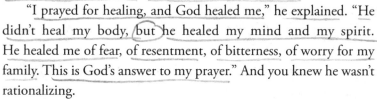

"I prayed for healing, and God healed me," he explained. "He didn't heal my body, but he healed my mind and my spirit. He healed me of fear, of resentment, of bitterness, of worry for my family. This is God's answer to my prayer." And you knew he wasn't rationalizing.

There is always the danger that a person who is zealous for healing will try to take the place of God in other people's lives. One man stayed at the bedside of a dying Christian leader for many hours. While he was out of the room for a brief period, the leader died. He blamed his absence for the death.

A month or so after our five-year-old died of leukemia, the same man—a sincere, well-educated Christian—told me that our son need not have died, if we had only possessed faith.

"Do you really believe that?" I asked.

"Yes, I do," he replied.

"Do you believe it enough to pray that your own child will become sick with leukemia so that you can prove your faith?"

After a long silence, he replied, "No, I don't."

I do not object to such zealots when they are dealing with other adults. I do object to the traumatic effect they may have on children and teenagers.

The summer after our eighteen-year-old son died, our sixteen-year-old daughter was at a Christian camp. A visiting minister, in the presence of and with the silent acquiescence of the camp director, told this grieving girl, "Your brother need not have died, if your parents had only had faith for his healing. It is not God's will for one to die before the age of sixty."

When our daughter told us this in a letter, I thought about One who died in his early thirties, One who loved children enough not to hurt them.

Joseph Tate Bayly (1920–1986) was an American author and publishing executive. His column, "Out of My Mind," was published in *Eternity* magazine from 1961 to 1986.

Unless otherwise indicated, Scripture references are from the *Revised Standard Version* of the Bible.

Scripture quotations marked KJV are from the *King James Version* of the Bible.

Part Two

AN AIM THAT KEEPS ME PRESSING ON

7

Finishing with Few Regrets

RANDY ALCORN

Endurance is Christ's call to follow him, to finish strong for God's glory. There is no higher calling, no bigger privilege, no greater joy. In the final analysis, endurance will be a measure of the kind of character and integrity we develop.

I asked a gathering of thousands, "How many of you, in five or ten or thirty years from now, want to be sold out to Jesus Christ, a disciple of the King, empowered by the Holy Spirit, saturated in his Word, and yielded to his will?" Ninety percent of the hands shot up. They meant it.

Then I told them the bad news—many who raised their hands would never become that person. They would not finish well. It's easier to raise a hand today than to make the kinds of choices day after day after day that result in a long obedience in the same direction.

Every day we are becoming someone—the question is, who? Author Jerry Bridges, hearing me address this, told me that Dawson Trotman, founder of the Navigators, used to say, "You are going to be what you are now becoming."

Scripture speaks of this process of character development: "And we all, with unveiled face, beholding the glory of the Lord, are being transformed into the same image from one degree of glory to another" (2 Cor. 3:18). You become like what you choose to behold. Behold Christ, and you become Christlike. Gaze upon superficiality and immorality, and it's equally predictable what you'll become.

Who you become will be the cumulative result of the daily choices you make. "The path of the righteous is like the light of dawn, which shines brighter and brighter until full day" (Prov. 4:18). This is why Scripture continually warns us against wrong choices: "Do not enter the path of the wicked and do not walk in the way of the evil. Avoid it; do not go on it; turn away from it and pass on" (Prov. 4:14–15).

Our choices flow out of our hearts, and therefore we must take care to guard them from contamination: "Above all else, guard your heart, for it is the wellspring of life" (Prov. 4:23 NIV). What's the most effective way to contaminate a water supply? Poison it at its source. If you don't guard your heart from the world's values, you will be conformed to the world (Rom. 12:1–2). It takes no more effort to be conformed to the world than it does to float downstream. To be transformed by the renewing of our minds is to swim upstream against the current. Renewing our minds requires conscious, deliberate effort.

You will become the product of what you choose to delight in and meditate upon. Psalm 1 is a powerful formula for endurance: "Blessed is the man who walks not in the counsel of the wicked, nor stands in the way of sinners, nor sits in the seat of scoffers, but his delight is in the law of the LORD, and on his law he meditates day and night."

We all meditate, and we're all shaped by the object of our meditation. We take our attitudinal and behavioral cues from it. This week, will I be shaped by situation comedies, soap operas, and newspapers, or will I be shaped by Isaiah, Luke, A. W. Tozer, and Charles Haddon Spurgeon? It depends on how I choose to spend my time.

Psalm 1 says the one who continually meditates on God's Word "is like a tree planted by streams of water that yields its fruit in its season, and its leaf does not wither." Trees don't choose where to place themselves, but we do. We determine what our sources of nourishment will be, which in turn determine whether we bear fruit or wither.

Following Christ isn't magic. It requires repeated actions on our part, which develop into habits and life disciplines. Christ-centered endurance doesn't just happen, any more than running a marathon or climbing a mountain just happens or having a good marriage just happens. Endurance requires a good plan, with clear and tangible steps that are taken one after the other. The farmer tills the soil. The weeds have to be removed. He doesn't say, "Lord, please remove the weeds." He prays, "Lord, give me your strength as I pull these weeds today." *daily*

The athlete doesn't say, "Lord, go out there and win that race." He says, "God, empower me to run hard and do my best, and if you so desire it, to win."

The key to spirituality is the development of little habits, such as Bible reading and memorization and prayer. In putting one foot in front of the other day after day, we become the kind of person who grows and endures rather than withers and dies.

Ten years from now, would you like to look back at your life, after you've made consistently good decisions about eating right and exercising regularly? Sure. But there's a huge gap between wishes and reality. The bridge over the gap is self-control, a fruit of the Spirit (Gal. 5:22–23). The key to self-control is discipline, which produces a long-term track record of small choices in which we yield to God's Spirit, resulting in new habits and lifestyles. Spirit-control and self-control are interrelated in Scripture, because godly self-control is a yielding of self to God's Spirit.

Most of us know the difference between eating cottage cheese and Krispy Kremes. Or the difference between a daily workout and spending life on a couch. Likewise, there's a difference between whether you read the Bible or you don't, whether you spend the evening watching *American Idol* or *Survivor* or reading the Bible or a great Christian book. While the difference today may seem small, the cumulative difference will be great.

We want the fruit of the spiritual disciplines, but often we're unwilling to do the work they actually require. We want the rewards without the sacrifices. The life of endurance requires us doing many hard things. But these hard things are the very ones that bring purpose, joy, and satisfaction to our lives.

Endurance requires a lifetime of yielding your body to the Holy Spirit. "Do not let sin reign in your mortal body so that you obey its evil desires. Do not *offer* the parts of your body to sin, as instruments of wickedness, but rather *offer* yourselves to God . . . and offer the parts of your body to him as instruments of righteousness" (Rom. 6:12–14 NIV)

What can we do without our bodies? That's the significance of Romans 12:1–2:

> *I urge you, brothers, in view of God's mercy, to offer your bodies as living sacrifices, holy and pleasing to God—this is your spiritual act of worship. Do not conform any longer to the pattern of this world, but be transformed by the renewing of your mind.* (NIV)

Notice the interrelation of mind and body. It's not just that we should renew our minds and expect that our bodies will follow. Rather, we offer our bodies to place ourselves where our minds can be renewed.

We use our hands to write the check and put it in the offering plate. Where we put our treasure through the physical discipline of giving, our hearts will follow (Matt. 6:21).

We open our mouths to share the gospel. We move our legs to

run from immorality. We avert our eyes to avoid looking at someone with lust.

Bodily actions open a Bible and turn off a television. To read a book or listen to God we have to make a concerted effort to turn our ears and eyes away from this loud, invasive world.

We're not only spiritual beings, we're physical. If we don't offer our bodies as living sacrifices, our minds won't be renewed. Why? Because our minds will only be fed and shaped by the input our bodies provide them.

Consider again Psalm 1:1–2. "Blessed is the man who walks not in the counsel of the wicked, nor stands in the way of sinners, nor sits in the seat of scoffers; but his delight is in the law of the LORD, and on his law he meditates day and night." In each case, there is a physical action— walk, stand, sit. To meditate on the Word involves opening it with our hands, looking at it with our eyes, or speaking it with our lips.

"Look carefully then how you walk, not as unwise but as wise, making the best use of the time" (Eph. 5:15–16). Why not redeem two hours of your day that you would have spent on television, newspaper, video games, phone, working overtime, or hobbies? Change your habits. Spend one hour meditating on and/or memorizing Scripture. Spend the other hour reading a great book. Share what you're learning with your spouse and children, or a friend. Listen to Scripture and audio books and praise music while you fold clothes, pull weeds, or drive. Say no to talk radio or sports radio, not because they're bad but because you have something better to do. Fast from television, radio, and the Internet for a week. Discover how much more time you have. Redeem that time by establishing new habits of cultivating your inner life and learning to abide in Christ. "I am the vine; you are the branches. Whoever abides in me and I in him, he it is that bears much fruit, for apart from me you can do nothing" (John 15:5).

Give Jesus first place in your life. Don't just let your life happen. Choose what to do with it, or in the end you'll wonder where it went. If you're going to persevere as Christ's follower, you must consciously choose not to squander your life or let it idle away, but to invest it in what matters.

Don't just let your life happen.
Choose what to do with it, or in the end
you'll wonder where it went.

One day we'll be with the Person we were made for, living in the Place we were made for. Joy will be the air we breathe. We will be forever grateful there for the persevering grace extended to us by Jesus, King of kings. We should remind ourselves regularly that the best is yet to be. We have yet to reach our peaks, and when we reach them in the resurrection, we will never pass them. This assurance will help us here and now to live self-controlled and disciplined lives of deferred gratification, knowing that eternal rewards await us in the presence of our Lord, the Headwaters of Eternal Joy.

January 2006 was the fiftieth anniversary of the death of the five missionaries martyred in Ecuador. That month in our church services I interviewed Steve Saint, son of Nate Saint, and Mincaye, one of the tribal warriors who killed the missionaries and later came to faith in Christ. One of Ed McCully's sons joined us when we were invited by Jim Elliot's family to have dinner in Portland at the house Jim grew up in.

There we were, with family members of three of the five martyrs, along with Mincaye, who is like family to them now. Also with us were Jim Elliot's older brother, Bert, and his wife, Colleen. In 1949, when Bert and Colleen were students at Multnomah Bible College, they were invited to Peru by a missionary. They became missionaries to Peru years before Jim went to Ecuador.

That January when we met them, they were on a furlough. When we were talking about Peru, Bert smiled and said, "I can't wait to get back." Now in their eighties, they're nearing their sixtieth year as missionaries. Until that weekend I didn't know anything about these people. Bert and Colleen Elliot will enter God's Kingdom "under the radar" of the church at large, but not under God's.

Bert said something to me that day I'll never forget: "Jim and I both served Christ, but differently. Jim was a great meteor, streaking through the sky."

Bert didn't finish by describing himself. But I'll describe him this way: a faint star that rises night after night and faithfully crosses the same path in the sky, unnoticed on earth, unlike his brother Jim, the shooting star.

I believe Jim Elliot is experiencing great reward. But I wouldn't be surprised to one day discover that Bert and Colleen Elliot's reward is even greater.

"Multitudes who sleep in the dust of the earth will awake: some to everlasting life, others to shame and everlasting contempt. Those who are wise will shine like the brightness of the heavens, and those who lead many to righteousness, like the stars for ever and ever" (Dan. 12:2–3 NIV).

Bert and Colleen Elliot have lived a long obedience in the same direction. Whether we follow God to leave our country or to stay here, all of us are likewise called to a life of faithful endurance, empowered by Christ.

Wouldn't it be great to get to the end of our lives with as few regrets as possible?

So let's ask ourselves, *when our life here is over, what will we wish we'd done less of and more of?*

In terms of character-building choices, why not ask God to empower you to spend the rest of your life closing the gap between what you'll wish you would have done and what you really have done?

Adapted from the chapter "Cumulative Daily Decisions, Courage in a Cause, and a Life of Endurance" by Randy Alcorn in the book, *Stand: A Call for the Endurance of the Saints,* © 2008 by Desiring God, published by Crossway.

Randy Alcorn is director of Eternal Perspective Ministries, a nonprofit Christian organization dedicated to teaching an eternal viewpoint and helping the needy of the world.

Unless otherwise indicated, all Scripture references are from the ESV® Bible (*The Holy Bible, English Standard Version®*).

Scripture quotations marked NIV are from *The Holy Bible: New International Version.*®

8

My Father Taught Me How to Die

R. C. SPROUL

Dare we think of death as a vocation? The author of Ecclesiastes made this declaration:

> To everything there is a season, a time for every purpose under heaven: a time to be born, and a time to die. (Eccles. 3:1–2a)

Likewise the writer of Hebrews says:

> And as it is appointed for men to die once, but after this the judgment. (Heb. 9:27)

Scripture speaks of death in terms of a "*purpose* under heaven" and of an "appointment." Death is a divine appointment. It is part of God's purpose in our lives. God calls each person to die. He is sovereign over all of life, including the final experience of life.

I am aware that there are teachers who tell us that God has nothing to do with death. Death is seen strictly as the fiendish device of the Devil. All pain, suffering, disease, and tragedy are blamed on the Evil One. God is absolved of any responsibility. This view is designed to make sure that God is absolved of blame for anything that goes wrong in this world. "God always wills healing," we are told. If that healing does not happen, then the fault lies with Satan—or with ourselves. Death, they say, is not the plan of God. It represents a victory for Satan over the realm of God.

Such views may bring temporary relief to the afflicted. But they are not true. They have nothing to do with biblical Christianity. In an effort to absolve God of any blame, they do so at the expense of God's sovereignty.

Yes, there is a Devil. He is our archenemy. He will do anything in his power to bring misery into our lives. But Satan is not sovereign. Satan does not hold the keys of death.

When Jesus appeared in a vision to John on the Isle of Patmos, he identified himself with these words:

> Do not be afraid; I am the First and the Last. I am He who lives, and was dead, and behold, I am alive forevermore. Amen. And I have the keys of Hades and of Death. (Rev. 1:17–18)

Jesus holds the keys to death. Satan cannot snatch those keys out of his hand. The grip of Christ is firm. He holds the keys because he owns the keys. All authority in heaven and on earth has been given to him. That authority includes all authority over life and all authority over death. The angel of death is at his beck and call.

Above all suffering and death stands the crucified and risen Lord. He has defeated the ultimate enemy of life. He has vanquished the power of death. He calls us to die, but that call is a call to obedience to the final transition of life. Because of Christ, death is not final. It is a passage from one world to the next.

I will never forget the last words my father spoke to me. We were seated together on the living room sofa. His body had been ravaged by three strokes. One side of his face was distorted by paralysis. His left eye and left lip drooped uncontrollably. He spoke to me with a heavy slur. His words were difficult to understand, but their meaning was crystal clear. He uttered these words: "I have fought the good fight, I have finished the race. I have kept the faith."

These were the last words he ever spoke to me. Hours later he suffered his fourth and final cerebral hemorrhage. I found him col-lapsed on the floor, a trickle of blood oozing from the corner of his mouth. He was comatose. Mercifully, he died a day and a half later without regaining consciousness.

While his last words to me were heroic, my last words to him were cowardly. I protested his words of premonition. I said rudely, "Don't say that, Dad!"

There are many things that I have said in my life that I desper-ately wish I had not said. None of my words are more shameful to me now than those. But words can no more be recalled than a speed-ing arrow after the bow string has snapped in full release.

My words were a rebuke to him. I refused to allow him the dignity of a final testimony to me. He knew he was dying. I refused to accept what he had already accepted with grace.

I was seventeen. I knew nothing of the business of dying. It was not a very good year. I watched my father die an inch at a time over a period of three years. I never heard him complain. I never heard him protest. He sat in the same chair day after day, week after week, year after year. He read the Bible with a large magnifying glass. I was blind to the anxieties that must have plagued him. He could not work. There was no income. No disability insurance. He sat there, waiting to die, watching his life savings trickle away with his own life.

> A good fight is a fight fought without hostility, without bitterness, without self-pity.

I was angry at God. My father was angry at no one. He lived out his last days faithful to his vocation. He fought the good fight. A good fight is a fight fought without hostility, without bitterness, without self-pity. I had never been in a fight like that.

When my father died I was not a Christian. Faith was something beyond my experience and beyond my understanding. When he said, "I have kept the faith," I missed the weight of his words. I shut them out. I had no idea that he was quoting the apostle Paul's final message to his beloved disciple, Timothy. His eloquent testimony was wasted on me at the time. But not now. Now I understand. Now I want to persevere as he persevered. I want to run the race and finish the course as he did before me. I have no desire to suffer as he suffered. But I want to keep the faith as he kept it.

If my father taught me anything, he taught me how to die. My father ran a race because God called him to run the race. He finished the course because God was with him through every obstacle. He kept the faith because the faith kept him.

Adapted from *Surprised by Suffering: The Role of Pain and Death in the Christian Life*, by R. C. Sproul, © 2009. Used by permission of Reformation Trust.

R. C. Sproul is a theologian and pastor, and is chairman of Ligonier Ministries.

All Scripture references are from *The New King James Version* of the Bible.

9

Spiritual Light Shining from Your Deathbed

ABRAHAM KUYPER

Surely there are soul-exalting, God-glorifying sickbeds; and it has happened more than once, that on his last sickbed a person was permitted, as a witness and prophet of the Lord, in the circle of his family to finish a spiritual work.

But he who deems this to be the rule, is mistaken. This is rather highly exceptional. And when you think of the numbers of those who formerly companied with you spiritually and have since departed, you will mostly find that they were taken away without much spiritual light shining out from their deathbed.

Whether in such moments we have to reproach ourselves with respect to this is a question every child of God has to decide in his own conscience. The Lord can bring upon us so violent a plague, terrifying our whole being and benumbing our mind in anxiety and pain that it goes on altogether outside of our soul. Yet, let no one be overconfident about this; for the cases are not infrequent, that the powerlessness of our faith in such moments is bitter fruit of lack of faith's operation, if not of consenting to sin against God, when we were in health.

It is certainly wrong when, in our sickbed that threatens to become our deathbed, the need of glorifying God before our dying does not become a burden of prayer. See it in the case of David. He lay prostrate with a deadly disease; the plague of a serious, dangerous sickness had come upon him; and spiritually he felt himself languid and useless. He could not battle it. The force of the disease was too overwhelming, and listless as a log he lay upon his sickbed.

It is certainly wrong when, in our sickbed
that threatens to become our deathbed,
the need of glorifying God before our dying
does not become a burden of prayer.

But however benumbed and clouded he felt himself to be, there rested in him still this one thing, that this miserable, spiritual barrenness was a hindrance to him. He thirsted before dying to have a least a few brief moments in which the violence of the plague would abate, spiritual self-perception would return, and he could refresh himself preparatory to commending his soul into God's hands.

So he came to pray; and as he prayed, tears ran down his face, and then he cried: "Hear my prayer, O LORD, and give ear unto my cry; hold not thy peace at my tears: O, my God, turn thee away from me, that I may refresh myself, before I go hence, and be no more" (Ps. 39:12 AT).

Of course this prayer of David's must not be misunderstood. It was in no wise an exclamation of unbelief after the manner of Job's wife, to curse God before he died. The whole thirty-ninth Psalm shows this differently. Everything in this psalm is the longing of a worn-out and desolate soul after the living God.

David realized that God was in the plague; that this violent sickness came not upon him by chance, but of God; that in that plague God himself distressed him; and for this reason he supplicated: Turn thee as the reproving God *externally* away from me, and as the spiritual Comforter come *internally* to me.

What this servant of God supplicated was not to die like a dog, but that before the end came he might have a moment of relief, before dying, to be permitted to refresh himself, and so with clear, bright consciousness of faith to go into eternity.

So this prayer speaks of energy of faith, and in our serious sicknesses this is what we have to learn from David. A child of God must *never* give up; but, however violent the plague becomes, always struggle against it with the elasticity of his spiritual life.

Not as though in himself he would have a certain provision of strength to keep it up till the end. Faith never knows of anything except weaknesses, that in those weaknesses the power and the work of the Holy Spirit may become manifest.

It makes all the difference whether in such moments you let go of the Holy Ghost, or whether inwardly you hold yourself fast to him. And this difference you see so frequently. You find those who lie down upon their sickbed like a log, and, if they complain, they only complain of what ails their body. But for the rest they have given up. They are indeed willing that one should pray for them, but they no longer pray themselves. They simply undergo what God puts upon them. There is no more effort in their faith to harness the sinew of faith. Of the glory of the work of the Mediator they see nothing more. Everything about them has become barren and dead. And so the days and night go by, till finally it goes to death with them. This is sinning upon one's deathbed. There is something in this of denial of Christ.

And that this is not necessary is shown not only by David, but has equally well been evident with many a person bitterly afflicted

69

and severely plagued, who in the face of everything, with heroic courage of faith, held on to the uttermost.

 Then it was mostly observed that this heroism of faith inworked upon the body and silenced complaint of pain, in quiet patience to endure what had to be suffered. And though all the waves and billows went over him, he yet raised up the head again from out those dreadful waves, until it was enough, and the Lord made an end of it. And God's angels rejoiced, and they who loved him and at his deathbed wept because of their sorrow, yet also thanked God, that they had witnessed this power of faith again.

Adapted from the chapter, "That I May Refresh Myself before I Go Hence" in *In the Shadow of Death: Meditations for the Sick-Room and the Death-Bed* by Abraham Kuyper. Translation from the Dutch ©1929 by John Hendrik De Vries, D. D., published by William B. Eerdmans.

Abraham Kuyper (1837–1920) was a Dutch politician, journalist, statesman, and theologian. He founded the Anti-Revolutionary Party and was prime minister of the Netherlands between 1901 and 1905.

Scripture quotations marked AT are from the author's translation.

10

A Witness in the Way We Die

JOHN EAVES

Life is not about us. Life is about Jesus and our witness for him in this world. It has taken me a lifetime to embrace this fundamental truth in all of its implications. It has also taken the same amount of time to recognize that our witness for Jesus is frequently manifested in our absolute weakest moments rather than when we are at full strength.

My weakest moment began this past April when tests revealed stage 4 metastatic cancer originating in the colon, simmering unde-tected for eight or nine years. Only recently had it apparently spread to other vital organs. There was never any mention of "cure" either. Rather, I was assigned to a category called "palliative care patient," which is a nice way of saying, "we can try to keep you comfortable and extend your days through chemo treatments. But we will never be able to heal you."

When I returned from New York City to Nashville after receiv-ing my terminal cancer diagnosis, I spent the first three weeks pre-paring to die. As weird as this sounds, I think it is one of the greatest gifts we can give to our family in preparing for our own death. Why stick them with second-guessing and arranging the details at the most tender and vulnerable time of grieving? Kay and I reviewed our financial situation and made adjustments to our wills with our financial planner and attorney. We signed over car titles and property. I contacted the funeral director and filled out all of the necessary paperwork ahead of time. I even wrote my own memorial service and distributed it to those participating in the service. Once I completed the task of preparing to die, I was totally freed up to live and to focus on the ministry God has given to me.

Kay and I were praying together one night. I was shocked by my prayer, because it was like someone else was praying it. I said, "Lord, I know there are a lot of ways we can be a witness for you. We can be a witness in your miracles you perform in our lives; we can be a witness in walking through trials and hardship; we can even be a witness in the way we die."

The next morning I returned to a favorite passage of mine—Hebrews 11:32–12:3. As you know, biblical scholars know this chapter as the roll call of faith. It is an attempt by the writer to look over our shoulders and remember all that God has done through his people over the centuries and of his faithfulness to us as his people. What I find fascinating about this passage is that in many ways it is the most realistic view of the Christian life in the Bible. Why? Because it presents life as it really is for a follower of Jesus rather than how we would want it to be—full of ease, prosperity, and blessing.

The first few sentences in the paragraph are predictable. Miracles are performed—the dead raised to life, people delivered from certain death. It is an incredibly powerful encounter with God when he breaks into human circumstance. Suddenly, the tone changes beginning in the second part of Hebrews 11:35. God's people are being openly violated, persecuted, tortured, beaten, and killed for their faith. They are deprived of earthly comforts, disoriented, and destitute. Many died, for no other reason than identifying themselves as servants of God and following his directives.

Could it be that we in America have been sold short when it comes to understanding the Christian life in the fullness it represents? Yes, we have. We seek the easy way. We forget that throughout biblical history, trials, hardship, and death are equally a part of our witness to an unbelieving world as are healing and deliverance and divine blessing.

As followers of Jesus, we embrace the miraculous. God loves to work with circumstances with labels like "impossible," "terminal," and "hopeless." In my case, I am very open handed with God healing me, even this very moment. There is absolutely no question in my mind that he can do it, and I am ready to receive this form of grace. But I don't demand it. I don't insist on my way being his way of handling my current circumstance. That is one foolish line of thinking—taking his promises he gave us and forcing his hand to do my bidding.

In the same manner, contrary to a lot of TV teaching on the issue of faith and healing, I also do not think my healing is solely about my faith and me. I do not think Jesus will have a conversation with me in heaven saying, "John, I would have healed you, but your faith quotient was only 48 percent and you needed a 50 percent minimum to pass," or "I would have healed you if you just would have gone to the Benny Hinn or Kenneth Hagin healing conference."

As I read the Scriptures, I notice something striking about Jesus and healing. Roughly half the time Jesus makes some comment regarding the faith of the person he has healed. But the other times, he just healed people with no precondition whatsoever.

Today there is a lot of bad teaching floating around on healing. One particularly devastating teaching is to have a person prayed over, healing claimed, and then nothing more be said about the illness.

I met such a woman a few months ago. Like me, she had terminal cancer. With tears in her eyes, she recounted how, as a mother of five children, she had undergone all kinds of alternate treatments in Mexico, four diets for cancer healing, and a multitude of other advice. "I simply cannot do this anymore," she said, "because I realize that everything I have tried is all about me. It is about how I am going to take control over my own healing. I just can't do that anymore. I told God I was at the end of my rope and gave it over to him."

key

I said to her, "That is not the end. It is the beginning. All this time, the Lord has wanted you to place this disease in his hands, not your own." I also told her that because of the poor teaching she had received on healing, her family was going to be the ones to suffer the most. It will be her kids who say, "Mommy died because we didn't have enough faith for mommy to be healed."

"Is that the kind of baggage you want to leave to your family?" I asked.

"No, but"

"No," she said. I thought it was a breakthrough. But several weeks later I learned she was back in Mexico at a clinic for alternate cancer treatments. How simple a transaction it is to put our life in God's hands, yet how complicated we make it by keeping our hands on the controls.

The right attitude about miracles and God's breaking into our lives is simply to trust him. This may sound too easy for you. Trust is the practical outworking of faith, and Jesus was the first to remind us of this important truth.

TRUST

Do you remember the conversation the disciples had with Jesus about who was the greatest in the kingdom of heaven? Jesus drew a child standing close to him in his arms, and said, "Unless you change and become like little children, you will never enter the kingdom of heaven" (Matt. 18:3). Jesus knew that without a complete reworking

EAVES | *A Witness in the Way We Die*

of our adult view of faith, we are hopelessly lost. And what is the essence of a childlike faith? Is it not unreserved trust?

Faith has two distinct expressions for the follower of Jesus. The first we can call an "active faith." It is a tenacious faith, holding on and holding out until God responds. The persistent widow is the poster child of this kind of faith, and Jesus himself uses her in a parable to teach us to persevere in our prayers and to not give up (Luke 18:1–8).

However, the second biblical expression of faith is equally viable and necessary. It is a "resting faith," a faith that knows . . . that it knows . . . that it knows. It is the faith we see expressed in Daniel 3:17–18 when Shadrach, Meshach, and Abednego said to the king of Babylon, "The God we serve is able to . . . rescue us from your hand, O king. But even if he does not . . . we will not serve your gods." It is the faith credited as righteousness to Abraham when he believed God for a son in his old age (Gen. 15:6). This is the faith God has imparted into my life. I am resting in his daily provision, never insisting on things going my way, but his. It is a yielded life, a surrendered life, which intimately becomes a transformed life (Rom. 8:28–30).

One of the great lessons I learned through my illness is that God will frequently call us to come alongside others who are facing the same circumstance we are. I call it "incarnational illness." God deliberately intersects our lives with the hurting at the very moment when we hurt. Why does he do this? Because he knows that weakness is the perfect soil for growing dependence in him. Stripped of our own gifts and resources, we are perfectly positioned to trust him.

I did not take chemotherapy because I thought it would help me. I had resolved in my heart to never suffer twice for the same disease. When chemo treatments became more painful than the cancer, that was to be my signal to stop. The day before my first treatment

75

I spent time walking and praying, and I distinctly sensed the Lord saying in my conscience, "This chemo is not about you. I want to get you closer to other cancer patients I want you to meet." The next day, my chemo nurse turned out to be a wonderful believer. She introduced me to three other men who had the exact diagnosis as I did. Chemo treatment centers can be unusual places. Some people want to hide; others just want to get it over with and get home. For me, the treatment center became my new congregation. Rather than hide behind curtains, we circled our chairs and began to talk. When I learned to unhook my infusion pump and let it run on batteries, I was able to meet new friends every time I went in for treatment.

I will never forget the hours after my first chemo treatment; I sank down in a chair in our living room, feeling absolutely miserable in twenty different ways. My twenty-one-year-old son came in and sat next to me. He asked, "Dad, would you teach me the Bible?" For those of you with children, you know how precious that moment was. He was looking at me through the eyes of an uncertain future and knew there was something I could tell him about this journey that he needed to know. In our weakest moments, God moves toward us and asks us to extend ourselves to others.

> In our weakest moments,
> God moves toward us and asks us to
> extend ourselves to others.

Contrary to popular belief, God does not place us on the sidelines of life when we walk through hardship. Rather, he takes us to the center of the playing field, so that the world can watch and observe his faithfulness in our lives.

God delivers his people in two ways: he delivers us *from* our trials, and he delivers us *through* our trials. The interesting thing is we do not have a choice as to which path we travel. Whether we experience his miracles of deliverance, endure hardship and trials, or even face death, we remain, now and forevermore, his witnesses. This is the essence of our life in him.

Adapted from the sermon, "Finishing Well: A Sermon on Learning to Live Through Terminal Illness" by John Eaves, given at West End Community Church, Nashville, Tennessee, November 23, 2003, and published in *Finishing Well: Learning to Live Through Terminal Illness* by John Eaves, ©2007 Kay Eaves. Used by permission.

John Eaves, who died in 2004, three months after this sermon was preached, was director of InterFACE (International Friendship Activities and Cultural Exchange) Ministries in Nashville, Tennessee.

Scripture references are from *The Holy Bible: New International Version.*®

11

Sickness: The Soul's Undressing

JEREMY TAYLOR

In sickness the soul begins to dress herself for immortality. First, she unties the strings of vanity that made her upper garment cleave to the world and sit uneasy; first, she puts off the light and fantastic summer robe of lust and wanton appetite; and as soon as that cestus, that lascivious girdle, is thrown away, then the reins chasten us, and give us warning in the night; then that which called us formerly to serve the manliness of the body, and the childishness of the soul, keeps us waking, to divide the hours with the intervals of prayer, and to number the minutes with our penitential groans. Then the flesh sets uneasily and dwells in sorrow. The spirit feels itself at ease, freed from the petulant solicitations of those passions which in health were as busy and restless as atoms in the sun, always dancing, and always busy, and never sitting down, till a sad night of grief and uneasiness draws the veil, and lets them die alone in secret dishonor.

Next to this, the soul, by the help of sickness, knocks off the fetters of pride and vainer complacencies. Then she draws the curtains, and stops the light from coming in, and takes the pictures down, those fantastic images of self-love and gay remembrances of vain opinion and popular noises. Then the spirit stoops into the sobrieties of humble thoughts, and feels corruption chiding the forwardness of fancy, and allaying the vapors of conceit and factious opinions. For humility is the soul's grave into which she enters, not to die, but to meditate some of its troublesome appendages. There she sees the dust, and feels the dishonors of the body, and reads the register of all its sad adherences; and then she lays by all her vain reflections, beating upon her crystal and pure mirror from the fancies of strength and beauty, and little decayed prettinesses of the body.

And when, in sickness, we forget all our knotty discourses of philosophy, and a syllogism makes our head ache, and we feel our many and loud talkings served no lasting end of the soul, no purpose that now we must abide by, and that the body is like to descend to the land where all things are forgotten, then she lays aside all her remembrances of applauses, all her ignorant confidences, and cares only to know "Christ Jesus and him crucified," to know him plainly, and with much heartiness and simplicity.

Next to these, as the soul is still undressing, she takes off the roughness of her great and little angers and animosities, and receives the oil of mercies and smooth forgiveness, fair interpretations and gentle answers, designs of reconcilement and Christian atonement in their places. For so did the wrestlers in Olympus; they stripped themselves of all their garments, and then anointed their naked bodies with oil, smooth and vigorous; with contracted nerves and enlarged voice they contended vehemently, till they obtained their victory or their ease; and a crown of olives, or a huge pity, was the reward of their fierce contentions.

Some wise men have said that anger sticks to a man's nature as inseparable as other vices do to the manner of fools, and that anger is never quite cured—but God, that hath found out remedies for all diseases, hath so ordered the circumstances of man, that in the worser sort of men anger and great indignation consume and shrivel into little peevishnesses and uneasy accents of sickness, and spend themselves in trifling instances; and in the better and more sanctified it goes off in prayers and alms and solemn reconcilement.

We may reckon sickness amongst good things, as we reckon rhubarb and aloes and childbirth and labor and obedience and discipline; these are unpleasant, and yet safe; they are troubles in order to blessings, or they are securities from danger, or the hard choices of a less and a more tolerable evil.

Sickness is in some sense eligible, because it is the opportunity and the proper scene of exercising some virtues. It is that agony in which men are tried for a crown. Place the man in a persecution, let him ride in a storm, let his bones be broken with sorrow, and his eyelids loosened with sickness, let his bread be dipped in tears, and all the daughters of music be brought low; let God commence a quarrel against him, and be bitter in the accents of his anger or his discipline; then God tries your faith. Can you, then, trust his goodness, and believe him to be a father, when you groan under his rod? Can you rely upon all the strange propositions of Scripture, and be content to perish if they be not true? Can you receive comfort in the discourses of death and heaven, of immortality and the resurrection, of the death of Christ and conforming to his sufferings?

There are but two great periods in which faith demonstrates itself to be a powerful and mighty grace; and they are persecution and the approaches of death. For in our health and clearer days it is easy to talk of putting trust in God; we readily trust him for life when we are in health; for provisions when we have fair revenues; and for deliverance when we are newly escaped. But let us come to sit upon the margent of our grave, and let a tyrant lean hard upon our fortunes and dwell upon our wrong, let the storm arise, and the keels toss till the cordage crack, or that all our hopes bulge under us and descend into the hollowness of sad misfortunes; then can you believe, when you neither hear, nor see, nor feel anything but objections?

This is the proper work of sickness: faith is then brought into the theatre, and so exercised, that if it abides but to the end of the contention we may see the work of faith which God will hugely crown.

And so God dresses us for heaven. He loves us struggling with a disease, and resisting the Devil, and contesting against the weaknesses of nature, and against hope to believe in hope, resigning ourselves to God's will, praying him to choose for us, and dying in all things but faith and its blessed consequences.

When sickness hath made the difficulty, then God's grace hath made a triumph, and by doubling its power hath created new proportions of a reward; and then shows its biggest glory, when it hath the greatest difficulty to master, the greatest weaknesses to support, the most busy temptations to contest with; for so God loves that his strength should be seen in our weakness and our danger. Happy is that state of life in which our services to God are the dearest and the most expensive.

Sickness hath some degrees of eligibility, at least by an after-choice; because to all persons which are within the possibilities and state of pardon it becomes a great instrument of pardon of sins. God very often smites with his rod of sickness that he may not forever be slaying the soul with eternal death. "I will visit their offenses with the rod, and their sin with scourges; nevertheless my loving-kindness will I not utterly take from him, nor suffer my truth to fail" (Ps. 89:32–33). And there is in the New Testament a delivering over to Satan, and a consequent buffeting, for the mortification of the flesh indeed, but that the soul may be saved in the day of the Lord. And to some persons the utmost process of God's anger reaches but to a sharp sickness, or at most but to a temporal death; and then the little momentary anger is spent, and expires in rest and a quiet grave. Origen, Saint Augustine, and Cassian say, concerning Ananias and Sapphira that they were slain with a sudden death, that by such a judgment their sin might be punished, and their guilt expiated, and their persons reserved for mercy in the day of judgment. And God cuts off many of his children from the land of the living; and yet, when they are numbered amongst the dead, he finds them in the Book of Life, written amongst those that shall live to him forever.

> God very often smites with his rod of sickness that he may not forever be slaying the soul with eternal death.

For when sickness, which is the condition of our nature, is called for with purposes of redemption; when we are sent to death to secure eternal life; when God strikes us that he may spare us— it shows that we have done things which he essentially hates; and therefore we must be smitten with the rod of God—but in the midst of judgment. God remembers mercy, and makes the rod to be medicinal, and, like the rod of God in the hand of Aaron, to shoot forth buds and leaves and almonds, hopes and mercies and eternal recompenses, in the day of restitution.

It is certain that sickness never is an evil but by our own faults, and if we will do our duty, we shall be sure to turn it into a blessing. If the sickness be great, it may end in death, and the greater it is the sooner; and if it be very little, it hath great intervals of rest; if it be between both, we may be masters of it, and by serving the ends of Providence serve also the perfective end of human nature, and enter into the possession of everlasting mercies.

Adapted from *Holy Dying* by Jeremy Taylor.

Jeremy Taylor (1613–1667) was a clergyman in the Church of England. He is sometimes known as the "Shakespeare of Divines" for his poetic style of expression.

Part Three

A HOPE
THAT SAVES ME
FROM DESPAIR

12

Rubbing Hope into the Reality of Death

TIMOTHY KELLER

I can say without fear of contradiction, that no matter who you are, there's a lot of death in your future. You're getting older. Either you'll face death yourself or you'll live a long time and face the deaths of those around you.

But I can also say that Christianity gives you something to deal with that death. Paul writes in 1 Thessalonians 4:13, "Brothers, we do not want you to be ignorant about those who fall asleep, or to grieve like the rest of men, who have no hope."

Paul is not saying that since you have hope you won't grieve. He's not suggesting you should be somewhere between hope and grief. He's suggesting an extreme balance. He's saying, "I want you to grieve, but not hopelessly. I want you to have hopeful grief."

First, he says, Christians grieve. The Bible doesn't suggest to us a stoic approach to death. The most remarkable example of grief in the face of death is Jesus himself at the tomb of Lazarus. Jesus didn't at all take the Victorian approach of keeping a stiff upper lip. When he gets to Mary, all he does is weep. And when he gets to the tomb of Lazarus, Jesus is quaking with rage. Even though he knew he was going to raise Lazarus from the dead, he is angry. Jesus is grieving and he's mad. over death

How could the Lord of his world be angry with something in his world? Because death is an intruder in his world. Death was not part of the original design. We were never meant to die; we were meant to last. We were meant to get more and beautiful with time, not more and more shriveled. We were meant to get stronger and stronger, not weaker and weaker. We were meant to get brighter and brighter, not to fade. Death wasn't part of the original design.

Jesus' response to death shows that death is a monstrosity, an abnormality. Paul says in Romans 8 that when we decided to be our own saviors and lords, everything in creation broke. Our bodies broke. The world broke. Life broke. Death is part of that.

When you say, "death is just natural," you're actually killing a part of your heart that is quintessentially human. You're killing something within you. You're killing hope. You know deep in your heart that you are not like a tree or grass. You want to last. The deepest desire of the heart is for a love that will last.

Here is the balance Paul is suggesting—take your anger and grief and rub hope into it, the way people used to have to rub salt into meat to keep it from going bad. Rub hope deep into your grief and it will make you wise.

Take your anger and grief and rub hope
into it . . . and it will make you wise.

Not to grieve kills your humanity. Just to rage kills your humanity. But to press hope into your grief makes you wise and compassionate. It makes you humble and tender.

Do you see how extreme and yet how balanced this is? Where do you get this fearless anger? Where do you get this freedom to scream and cry out, and at the same time, a firm sense that death is a defeated enemy? How do you get that balance?

What does Paul mean when says he doesn't want us to grieve "like the rest of men who have no hope" since almost all other religions and cultures have some sort of hope for what comes after death? The answer, Paul says, is to embrace the uniquenesses of your hope.

He says, "I want you to think about how the Christian hope is overwhelmingly greater than any other hope offered. I want you to contrast the Christian hope with the others offered out there so you will take hold of and appropriate what is offered to you in Christ." How is the Christian hope unique?

First, the Christian hope is for a world of infinite love. There are plenty of religions and cultures that say there is life after death, but in them you lose your personal consciousness; you lose your individuality, which was an illusion anyway. You're like a drop going back in the ocean.

Paul is saying, "I want you to see that Christian hope is a future of love." In this passage in 1 Thessalonians, he repeatedly talks about being "together." But even more important than being with each other is his emphasis on being with Christ.

In verse 15 Paul speaks of those "who are left till the coming of the Lord." The Greek uses the word *parsea*, which is a hard word to translate. Sometimes it's translated "appearing of the Lord" rather than "coming of the Lord." In the Greek it is usually used to refer to a great personage, a king or an emperor. What it's really saying is that what we are looking forward to is not just the coming of the Lord or the appearing of the Lord, but the getting of the Lord personally. It is speaking of an intimate, face-to-face knowing.

Nobody who knows you completely can love you completely. There are people who think you're great because they don't really know you. There is nobody on the face of the earth who could know you to the bottom and love you to the skies. But we want that.

When someone likes you but doesn't know you, it's not that satisfying. And when someone knows you and doesn't like you, that certainly isn't satisfying. What we want is to be utterly known and utterly loved.

And on that day, at the coming of the Lord, we'll finally get what we've longed for—from him and one another. We'll be utterly known and utterly loved. Yes, the future is a world of love, the kind of love you want, a personal love.

2, Secondly, the Christian hope is a hope that you are going to get the life you always wanted. Death is not really defeated if, when you die, you simply go to be in heaven. Look at what death does to the body. Just to say that we'll be free and enter into an immaterial world is not the defeat of death. Our Christian hope is that we're going to live with Christ in a new earth, where there is not only no more death, but where life is what it was always meant to be. a new garden

Notice that 1 Thessalonians 4 says the Lord will come from heaven and have with him all who have died in Christ. Then it says we will be "caught up" to meet the Lord in the air and we will be forever with the Lord. But it doesn't really say what we will do then. It kind of leaves us hanging—literally. What then?

This passage has been misunderstood and I can see why. Most people assume it means, "and then we go to be in heaven forever," what is often called "the rapture." That's not what it means. The word for "meet" in the Greek was a term for people coming out of the city and joining the entourage of a conquering king who was coming in.

Imagine the king of your city had gone out and was coming back with the spoils of war. Instead of waiting for him to come back into your city, you would go outside the city to meet him and walk into city with him and therefore participate in his victory.

This passage is not saying that we are being caught up and taken out of the world into heaven. It means that we are being caught up with him on his way to earth to make it everything it ought to be, and will participate in his victory.

Our future is not that we will live in an ethereal, immaterial world. You're not going to float around in the kingdom of God. You're going to eat; you're going to love. You're going to sing because you'll have vocal chords! In realms and degrees of joy, satisfaction, and power that you cannot now imagine, you're going to eat and drink with the Son of Man. On that day we're going to see each other and say, "I always knew you could be like this. I saw glimpses of it, flashes of it, and now, look at you!" You're going to get the life you always wanted. This is only the real defeat of death.

So the Christian hope, in distinction from the religions and cultures that offer you an impersonal future, gives you a world of love. In distinction from religions that give you an ethereal, immaterial future, the Christian hope gives you the life you've always wanted. Lastly, while other religions and cultures talk about an afterlife, none gives you the assurance of it.

The word *hope*, as it is used in the Bible, doesn't really mean what our English word means. It means a life shaping, joyous certainty of something.

Paul says to the Thessalonians, "For God did not appoint us to suffer wrath but to receive salvation through our Lord Jesus Christ" (1 Thess. 5:9). Notice that he is speaking in the past tense. He doesn't say, "God might appoint you if you live a good enough life."

Paul is saying, "You've already been appointed to that. You've been appointed to be loved. You've been appointed to be known to the bottom, but loved to the sky."

How can that be?

It says, "He died for us so that, whether we are awake or asleep, we may live together with him" (1 Thess. 5:10). Jesus took the wrath. He died for us. The sting of death is sin and the poison went into Jesus.

The Bible doesn't say, "Don't fear death because it's natural." The Bible says, "Don't fear death because it's been defeated."

If you are not at home in a universe of death, that means you were actually built for something else. The Christian hope offers the assurance of that future. Our character and daily life are shaped by what we believe about our ultimate future.

Paul says, "You are all sons of the light and sons of the day" (1 Thess. 5:5). In other words, the day is coming when Jesus will make this material universe new. So live in the reality of that day. Grieve with confident hope in that coming day. Live in this world of death in the light of that future light.

Adapted from the sermon "Death and the Christian Hope" by Timothy Keller, given at Redeemer Presbyterian Church on April 4, 2004, ©2009 by Timothy Keller. All rights reserved. Used by permission.

Timothy Keller is founding pastor of Redeemer Presbyterian Church in New York, New York.

Scripture references are from *The Holy Bible: New International Version.*®

13

Hope Is a Glorious Grace

JOHN OWEN

Hope is a glorious grace, whereunto blessed effects are ascribed in the Scripture, and an effectual operation unto the supportment and consolation of believers. By it are we purified, sanctified, saved. And, to sum up the whole of its excellency and efficacy, it is a principal way of the working of Christ as inhabiting in us: "Christ in you, the hope of glory" (Col. 1:27). Where Christ evidences his presence with us, he gives us an infallible hope of glory; he gives us an assured pledge of it, and works our souls into an expectation of it.

Christ . . . gives us an infallible hope of glory;
he gives us an assured pledge of it,
and works our souls into an expectation of it.

Hope in general is but an uncertain expectation of a future good which we desire; but as it is a gospel of grace, all uncertainty is removed from it, which would hinder us of the advantage intended in it. It is an earnest expectation, proceeding from faith, trust, and confidence, accompanied with longing desires of enjoyment. From a mistake of its nature, it is that few Christians labor after it, exercise themselves unto it, or have the benefit of it; for to live by hope,

93

they suppose, infers a state not only beneath the life of faith and all assurance in believing, but also exclusive of them. They think to hope to be saved is a condition of men who have no grounds of faith or assurance; but this is to turn a blessed fruit of the Spirit into a common affection of nature. Gospel hope is a fruit of faith, trust, and confidence; yea, the height of the actings of all grace issues in a well-grounded hope, nor can it rise any higher (Rom. 5:2–5).

Now, the reason why men have no more use of, no more benefit by, this excellent grace, is because they do not abide in thoughts and contemplation of the things hoped for. The especial object of hope is eternal glory (Rom. 5:2; Col. 1:27). The peculiar use of it is to support, comfort, and refresh the soul in all trials, under all weariness and despondencies, with a firm expectation of a speedy entrance into that glory, with an earnest desire after it. Wherefore, unless we acquaint ourselves by continual meditation with the reality and nature of this glory, it is impossible it should be the object of a vigorous, active hope, such as whereby the Apostle says "we are saved." Without this we can neither have that evidence of eternal things, nor that valuation of them, nor that preparedness in our minds for them, as should keep us in the exercise of gracious hope about them.

Suppose sundry persons engaged in a voyage unto a most remote country, wherein all of them have an apprehension that there is a place of rest and an inheritance provided for them. Under this apprehension they all put themselves upon their voyage, to possess what is so prepared. Howbeit some of them have only a general notion of these things. They know nothing distinctly concerning them and are so busied about other affairs that they have no leisure to inquire into them; or do suppose that they cannot come unto any satisfactory knowledge of them in particular, and so are content to go on with general hopes and expectations. There are others who by all possible means acquaint themselves particularly with the nature of the climate where they are going, with the excellency of the inheritance and provision that is made for them. Their voyage proves long and wearisome, their difficulties many, and their dangers great, and they have nothing to relieve and encourage themselves with but the hope and expectation of the country where they are going. Those of the first sort will be very apt to despond and faint; their general hopes will not be able to relieve them. But those who have a distinct notion and apprehension of the state of things where they are going, and of their incomparable excellency, have always in a readiness wherewith to cheer their minds and support themselves.

In that journey or pilgrimage wherein we are engaged towards a heavenly country, we are sure to meet with all kinds of dangers, difficulties, and perils. It is not a general notion of blessedness that will excite and work in us a spiritual, refreshing hope. But when we think and meditate on future glory as we ought, that grace which is neglected for the most part as unto its benefit, and dead as unto its exercise, will of all others be most vigorous and active, putting itself forth on all occasions. This, therefore, is an inestimable benefit of the duty exhorted unto, and which they find the advantage of who are really spiritually minded.

Adapted from "The Grace and Duty of Being Spiritually Minded" by John Owen. John Owen (1616–1683) was an English Nonconformist church leader and theologian. Scripture references are from the *King James Version* of the Bible.

14

Directions for a Peaceful Departure

RICHARD BAXTER

Comfort is not desirable only as it pleases us, but also as it strengthens us, and helps us in our greatest duties. And when is it more needful than in sickness, and the approach of death? I shall therefore add such directions as are necessary to make our departure comfortable or peaceful at the least, as well as safe.

Misunderstand not sickness, as if it were a greater evil than it is; but observe how great a mercy it is, that death has so suitable a harbinger or forerunner: that God should do so much before he takes us hence, to wean us from the world, and make us willing to be gone; that the unwilling flesh has the help of pain; and that the senses and appetite languish and decay, which did draw the mind to earthly things: and that we have so loud a call, and so great a help to true repentance and serious preparation! I know to those that have walked very close with God, and are always ready, a sudden death may be a mercy; as we have lately known diverse holy ministers and others, that have died either after a sacrament, or in the evening of the Lord's Day, or in the midst of some holy exercise, with so little pain, that none about them perceived when they died. But ordinarily it is a mercy to have the flesh brought down and weakened by painful sickness, to help to conquer our natural unwillingness to die.

Remember whose messenger sickness is, and who it is that calls you to die. It is he that is the Lord of all the world, and gave us the lives which he takes from us; and it is he that must dispose of angels and men, of princes and kingdoms, of heaven and earth; and therefore there is no reason that such worms as we should desire to be excepted. You cannot deny him to be the disposer of all things, without denying him to be God: it is he that loves us, and never meant us any harm in any thing that he has done to us; that gave the life of his Son to redeem us; and therefore thinks not life too good for us. Our sickness and death are sent by the same love that sent us a Savior, and sent us the powerful preachers of his Word, and sent us his Spirit, and secretly and sweetly changed our hearts, and knit them to himself in love; which gave us a life of precious mercies for our souls and bodies, and has promised to give us life eternal; and shall we think, that he now intends us any harm? Cannot he turn this also to our good, as he has done many an affliction which we have complained about?

Look by faith to your dying, buried, risen, ascended, glorified Lord. Nothing will more powerfully overcome both the poison and the fears of death, than the believing thoughts of him that has triumphed over it. Is it terrible as it separates the soul from the body? So it did by our Lord, who yet overcame it. Is it terrible as it lays the body in the grave? So it did by our Savior; though he saw not corruption, but quickly rose by the power of his Godhead. He died to teach us believingly and boldly to submit to death. He was buried, to teach us not overmuch to fear a grave. He rose again to conquer death for us, and to assure those who rise to newness of life, that they shall be raised at last by his power unto glory; and being made partakers of the first resurrection, the second death shall have no power over them. He lives as our head, that we might live by him; and that he might assure all those that are here risen with him, and seek first the things that are above, that though in themselves they are dead, yet their "life is hid with Christ in God; and when Christ who is our life, shall appear, then shall [we] also appear with him in glory" (Col. 3:3–5). What a comfortable word is that, John 14:19, "Because I live, ye shall live also."

Death could not hold the Lord of life; nor can it hold us against his will, who has the "keys of death and of Hades" (Rev. 1:18). He loves every one of his sanctified ones much better than you love an eye, or a hand, or any other member of your body, which you are not willing to lose if you are able to save it. When he ascended, he left us that message full of comfort for his followers in John 20:17, "Go to my brethren, and say unto them, I ascend unto my Father, and your Father; to my God, and your God" (KJV). Which, with these two following, I would have written before me on my sick bed. "If any man serve me, let him follow me; and where I am, there also shall my servant be" (John 12:26 KJV). And, "Verily, I say unto you, to-day shall you be with me in paradise" (Luke 23:43). Oh what a joyful thought should it be to a believer, to think when he is dying, that he is going to his Savior, and that our Lord is risen and gone before us, to prepare a place for us, and take us in season to himself (John 14:2–4. "As you believe in God, believe thus in Christ; and then your hearts will be less troubled" [v.1]). It is not a stranger that we talk of to you; but your Head and Savior, that loves you better than you love yourselves, whose office it is there to appear continually for you before God, and at last to receive your departing souls; and into his hand it is, that you must then commend them, as Stephen did (Acts 7:59).

Choose out some promises most suitable to your condition, and roll them over and over in your mind, and feed and live on them by faith. If he be most troubled with the greatness of his sin, let it be such as . . . "For I will be merciful unto their unrighteousness, and their sins and iniquities will I remember no more" (Heb. 8:12

KJV). If it be the weakness of his grace that troubles him, let him choose "All that the Father gives me, shall come to me, and him that comes to me, I will in no wise cast out" (John 6:37). If it be the fear of death, and strangeness to the other world, that troubles you, remember the words of Christ before cited, and 2 Corinthians 5:8, "We are confident, and willing rather to be absent from the body, and present with the Lord." Fix upon some such word or promise, which may support you in your extremity.

Choose out some promises most suitable
to your condition, and roll them over and over
in your mind, and feed and live on them
by faith.

Look up to God, who is the glory of heaven, and the light, and life, and joy of souls, and believe that you are going to see his face, and to live in the perfect, everlasting fruition of his fullest love among the glorified. The infant that newly comes out of the womb into this illuminated world of human converse, receives not such a joyful change as the soul that is newly loosed from the flesh, and passes from this mortal life to God. One sight of God by a blessed soul, is worth more than all the kingdoms of the earth. It is pleasant to the eyes to behold the sun; but the sun is darkness and useless compared to his glory.

Oh that God would make us foreknow by a lively faith, what it is to behold him in his glory, and to dwell in perfect love and joy, and then death would no more be able to dismay us, nor should we be unwilling of such a blessed change!

Look up to the blessed society of angels and saints with Christ, and remember their blessedness and joy, and that you also belong to the same society, and are going to be numbered with them. It will greatly overcome the fears of death, to see by faith the joys of them that have gone before us. Is not their company desirable? God will be all in all there to us, as the only sun and glory of that world; and yet we shall have pleasure, not only to see our glorified Redeemer, but also to converse with the heavenly society, and to sit down with Abraham, Isaac, and Jacob in the kingdom of God, and to love and praise him in consort and harmony with all those holy, blessed spirits. And shall we be afraid to follow, where the saints of all generations have gone before us? And shall the company of our best, and most, and happiest friends, be no inducement to us? Though it must be our highest joy to think that we shall dwell with God, and next that we shall see the glory of Christ, yet is it no small part of my comfort to consider that I shall follow all those holy persons whom I once conversed with that are gone before me.

That sickness and death may be comfortable to you, as your passage to eternity, take notice of the seal and earnest of God, even the Spirit of grace which he has put into your heart. The very love of holiness and holy persons, and your desires to know God and perfectly love him, do show that heavenly nature or spirit within you, which is your surest evidence for eternal life. For that spirit was sent from heaven to draw up your hearts and fit you for it; and God does not give you such natures, and desires, and preparations in vain. God would not have given us a heavenly nature or desire, if he had not intended us for heaven.

Look also to the testimony of a holy life, since grace has employed you in seeking after the heavenly inheritance. It is unlawful and perilous to look after any works or righteousness of your own, so as to set it in whole or in part instead of Christ, or to ascribe to it any honor that is proper to him; as to imagine that you are innocent, or have fulfilled the law, or have made God a compensation by your merits or sufferings, for the sin you have committed; but yet you must judge yourselves on your sick beds as near as you can as God will judge you. If you say, But I have been a grievous sinner! I answer, so was Paul that yet rejoiced after in this evidence! Are not those sins repented of and pardoned? If you say, But I cannot look back upon a holy life with comfort, it has been so blotted and uneven! I answer, has it not been sincere, though it was imperfect? Did you not first seek "the kingdom of God, and his righteousness" (Matt. 6:33 KJV)? If you say, My whole life has been ungodly, till now at last that God has humbled me; I answer, it is not the length of time, but the sincerity of your hearts and service, that is your evidence. If you came in at the last hour, if now you are faithfully devoted to God, you may look with comfort on this change at last, though you must look with repentance on your sinful lives.

Look back upon all the mercies of your lives, and think whence they came and what they signify. Love tokens are to draw your hearts to him that sent them; these are dropped from heaven, to entice you there! If God has been so good to you on earth, what will he be in glory! If he so blessed you in this wilderness, what will he do in the land of promise! The sense of mercy will banish the fears and misgivings of the heart.

Remember (if you have attained to a declining age) what a competent time you have had already in the world. When I think how many years of mercy I have had, candor forbids me to grudge at the season of my death, and makes me almost ashamed to ask for longer life. How long would you stay, before you would be willing to come to God? If he desired our company no more than we do his, and desired our happiness in heaven no more than we desire it ourselves, we should linger here as Lot in Sodom! Must we be snatched away against our wills, and carried by force to our Father's presence?

Remember that all mankind are mortal, and you are to go no other way than all that ever came into the world have gone before you (except Enoch and Elias). Remember both how vile your body is, and how great an enemy it has proved to your soul; and then you will the more patiently bear its dissolution. It is not your dwelling house, but your tent or prison, that God is pulling down. And yet even this vile body, when it is corrupted, shall at last be changed "into the likeness of Christ's glorious body, the working of his irresistible power" (Phil. 3:20, 21). And it is a flesh that has so rebelled against the spirit, and made your way to heaven so difficult, and put the soul to so many conflicts, that we should more easily submit it to the will of justice, and let it perish for a time, when we are assured that mercy will at last recover it.

Remember what a world it is that you are to leave, and compare it with that which you are going to; and compare the life which is near an end, with that which you are next to enter upon. Was it not Enoch's reward when he had walked with God, to be taken to him from a polluted world? While you are here, you are yourselves defiled; sin is in your natures, and your graces are all imperfect; sin is in your lives, and your duties are all imperfect; you cannot be free from it one day or hour. And is it not a mercy to be delivered from it? Is it not desirable to you to sin no more? And to be perfect in holiness? To know God and love him as much and more than you can now desire? You are here every day lamenting your darkness, and unbelief, and estrangedness from God, and lack of love to him. How oft have you prayed for a cure of all this! And now would you not have it, when God would give it you?

Has God on purpose made the world so bitter to us, and permitted it to use us unjustly and cruelly, and all to make us love it less, and to drive home our hearts unto himself? And yet are we so unwilling to be gone?

Be fortified against all the temptations of Satan by which he uses to assault men in their extremity: stand it out in the last conflict, and the crown is yours.

Adapted from Richard Baxter's sermon "Directions for a Peaceful Death."

Richard Baxter (1615–1691) was an English Puritan church leader and theologian.

Scripture quotations marked KJV are from the *King James Version* of the Bible.

15

What More Should God Do to Persuade You to Accept Death Willingly?

MARTIN LUTHER

Since everyone must depart, we must turn our eyes to God, to whom the path of death leads and directs us. Here we find the beginning of the narrow gate and of the straight path to life (Matt. 7:14). All must joyfully venture forth on this path, for though the gate is quite narrow, the path is not long. Just as an infant is born with peril and pain from the small abode of its mother's womb into this immense heaven and earth, that is, into this world, so man departs this life through the narrow gate of death. And although the heavens and the earth in which we dwell at present seem large and wide to us, they are nevertheless much narrower and smaller than the mother's womb in comparison with the future heaven.

Death looms so large and is terrifying because our foolish and fainthearted nature has etched its image too vividly within itself and constantly fixes its gaze on it. Moreover, the Devil presses man to look closely at the gruesome mien and image of death to add to his worry, timidity, and despair. Indeed he conjures up before man's eyes all the kinds of sudden and terrible death ever seen and heard, or read by man. And then he also slyly suggests the wrath of God with which he (the Devil), in days past, now and then tormented and destroyed sinners. In that way he fills our foolish human nature with the dread of death while cultivating a love and concern for life, so that burdened with such thoughts, man forgets God, flees and abhors death, and thus, in the end is and remains disobedient to God.

We should familiarize ourselves with death during our lifetime, inviting death into our presence when it is still at a distance and not on the move. At the time of dying, however, this is hazardous and useless, for then death looms large of its own accord. In that hour we must put the thought of death out of mind and refuse to see it, as we shall hear. The power and might of death are rooted in the fearfulness of our nature and in our untimely and undue viewing and contemplating of it.

Sin also grows large and important when we dwell on it and brood over it too much. This is increased by the fearfulness of our conscience, which is ashamed before God and accuses itself terribly. That is the water that the Devil has been seeking for his mill. He makes our sins seem large and numerous. He reminds us of all who have sinned and of the many who were damned for lesser sins than ours so as to make us despair or die reluctantly, thus forgetting God and being found disobedient in the hour of death. This is true especially since man feels that he should think of his sins at that time and that it is right and useful for him to engage in such contemplation. That is not the fitting time to meditate on sin. That must be done during one's lifetime. During our lifetime, when we should constantly have our eyes fixed on the image of death, sin, and hell— as we read in Psalm 51:3, "My sin is ever before me"—the Devil closes our eyes and hides these images. But in the hour of death when our eyes should see only life, grace, and salvation, he at once opens our eyes and frightens us with these untimely images so that we shall not see the true ones.

You must look at death while you are alive and see sin in the light of grace, and hell in the light of heaven, permitting nothing to divert you from that view. You must resolutely turn your gaze, the thoughts of your heart, and all your senses, to look at death closely and untiringly only as seen in those who died in God's grace and who have overcome death, particularly in Christ, and then also in all his saints.

In such pictures death will not appear terrible and gruesome. No, it will seem contemptible and dead, slain and overcome in life. For Christ is nothing other than sheer life, as his saints are likewise. The more profoundly you impress that image upon you heart and gaze upon it, the more the image of death will pale and vanish of itself without struggle or battle. Thus your heart will be at peace and you will be able to die calmly in Christ and with Christ, as we read in Revelation 14:13, "Blessed are they who die in the Lord Christ."

This was foreshown in Numbers 21 where we hear that when the children of Israel were bitten by fiery serpents they did not struggle with these serpents, but merely had to raise their eyes to the dead bronze serpent and the living serpents dropped from them by themselves and perished. Thus you must concern yourself solely with the death of Christ and then you will find life. But if you look at death in any other way, it will kill you with great anxiety and anguish. This is why Christ says, "In the world—that is, in yourselves—you have unrest, but in me you will find peace" (John 16:33).

You must look at sin only within the picture of grace. Engrave that picture in yourself with all your power and keep it before your eyes. The picture of grace is nothing else but that of Christ on the cross and of all his dear saints.

How is that to be understood? Grace and mercy are there where

Christ on the cross takes your sin from you, bears it for you, and destroys it. To believe this firmly, to keep it before your eyes and not to doubt it, means to view the picture of Christ and to engrave it in yourself.

What more should God do to persuade you to accept death willingly and not to dread but to overcome it? In Christ he offers you the image of life, of grace, and of salvation so that you may not be horrified by the images of sin, death, and hell. Furthermore, he lays your sin, your death, and your hell on his dearest Son, vanquishes them, and renders them harmless for you. In addition, he lets the trials of sin, death, and hell that come to you also assail his Son and teaches you how to preserve yourself in the midst of these and how to make them harmless and bearable. And to relieve you of all doubt, he grants you a sure sign, namely, the holy sacraments. He commands his angels, all saints, all creatures, to join him in watching over you, to be concerned about your soul, and to receive it. He commands you to ask him for this and to be assured of fulfillment. What more can or should he do?

> In Christ [God] offers you the image of life,
> of grace, and of salvation so that you may
> not be horrified by the images of sin,
> death, and hell.

From this you can see that he is a true God and that he performs great, right, and divine works for you. Why, then, should he not impose something big upon you (such as dying), as long as he adds to it great benefits, help, and strength, and thereby wants to test the power of his grace. Thus we read in Psalm 111:2, "Great are the works of the LORD, selected according to his pleasure." Therefore, we ought to thank him with a joyful heart for showing us such wonderful, rich, and immeasurable grace and mercy against death, hell, and sin, and to laud and love his grace rather than fearing death so greatly.

Love and praise make dying very much easier, as God tells us through Isaiah, "For the sake of my praise I restrain it [wrath] for you, that I may not cut you off" (48:9). To that end may God help us. Amen.

Adapted from "A Sermon on Preparing to Die" by Martin Luther.

Martin Luther (1483–1546) was a German monk, theologian, and church Reformer whose ideas sparked the Protestant Reformation and changed the course of Western civilization.

16

Comfort against Fears of the Dying Hour

THOMAS BOSTON

You who are in Christ, who are true Christians, have hope in your end; and such a hope as may comfort you against all those fears which arise from the consideration of a dying hour.

Case 1: *"The prospect of death," will some of the saints say, "is uneasy to me, not knowing what shall become of my family when I am gone."*

Answer: The righteous has hope in his death, as to his family, as well as himself. Although you have little, for the present, to live upon; which has been the condition of many of God's chosen ones, 1 Corinthians 4:11 (KJV), "We," namely, the apostles, "both hunger, and thirst, and are naked, and are buffeted, and have no certain dwellingplace"; and though you have nothing to leave them, as was the case of that son of the prophets, who feared the Lord, and yet died in debt which he was unable to pay, as his poor widow represents (2 Kings 4:2); yet you have a good Friend to leave them to; a covenant God, to whom you may confidently commit them. "Leave thy fatherless children, I will preserve them alive; and let thy widows trust in me" (Jer. 49:11 KJV).

The world can bear witness of signal settlements made upon

the children of providence; such as by their pious parents have been cast upon God's providential care. It has been often remarked, that they lacked neither provision nor education. Moses is an eminent instance of this. He, though he was an outcast infant (Ex. 2:3) became learned in all the wisdom of the Egyptians (Acts 7:22) and became king in Jeshurun (Deut. 33:5). O! May we not be ashamed, that we do not confidently trust him with the concerns of our families, to whom, as our Savior and Redeemer, we have committed our eternal interests?

Case 2: *Death will take us away from our dear friends; yes, we shall not see the Lord in the land of the living, in the blessed ordinances.*

Answer: It will take you to your best Friend, the Lord Christ. The friends you leave behind you, if they be indeed people of worth, you will meet again, when they come to heaven, and you will never be separated anymore. If death takes you away from the temple below, it will carry you to the temple above. It will indeed take you from the streams, but it will set you down by the fountain. If it puts out your candle, it will carry you where there is no night, where there is an eternal day.

Case 3: *I have so much to do, in time of health, to satisfy myself as to my interest in Christ, about my being a real Christian, a regenerate man, that I judge it is almost impossible I should die comfortably.*

Answer: If it is thus with you, then double your diligence to make your calling and election sure. Endeavor to grow in knowledge, and walk closely with God—be diligent in self-examination; and pray earnestly for the Holy Spirit, whereby you may know the things freely given you of God. If you are enabled, by the power and Spirit of Christ, thus diligently to prosecute your spiritual concerns, though the time of your life be neither day nor night, yet at evening time it may be light.

Many weak Christians indulge doubts and fears about their

spiritual state, as if they placed at least some part of religion in their imprudent practice; but towards the end of life, they think and act in another manner. The traveler, who reckons that he has time to spare, may stand still debating with himself whether this or the other be the right way—but when the sun begins to set, he is forced to lay aside his scruples and resolutely to go forward in the road which he judges to be the right one, lest he lie all night in the open fields. Thus some Christians, who perplex themselves much throughout the course of their lives, with jealous doubts and fears, content themselves when they come to die with such evidences of the safety of their state as they could not be satisfied with before; and by disputing less against themselves, and believing more, court the peace they formerly rejected, and gain it too.

Case 4: *I am under a sad decay, in respect of my spiritual condition.*

Answer: Bodily consumptions may make death easy—but it is not so in spiritual decays. I will not say that a godly man cannot be easy in such a case, when he dies, but I believe it is rarely so. Ordinarily, I suppose a cry comes to awaken sleeping virgins, before death comes. Samson is set to grind in the prison, until his locks grow again. David and Solomon fell under great spiritual decays; but before they died, they recovered their spiritual strength and vigor. However, bestir yourselves without delay, to strengthen the things that remain—your fright will be the less, for being awakened from spiritual sleep before death comes to your bedside—and you ought to lose no time, seeing you know not how soon death may seize you.

Case 5: *It is terrible to think of the other world, that world of spirits, which I have so little acquaintance with.*

Answer: Your best friend is Lord of that other world. Abraham's bosom is kindly even to those who never saw his face. After death, your soul becomes capable of converse with the blessed inhabitants of that other world. The spirits of just men made perfect were once such as your spirit now is. And as for the angels, however superior their nature in the rank of beings, yet our nature is dignified above theirs, in the man Christ, and they are all of them your Lord's servants, and so your fellow servants.

Case 6: *The pangs of death are terrible.*

Answer: Yet not so terrible as pangs of conscience, caused by a piercing sense of guilt, and apprehensions of divine wrath, with which I suppose them to be not altogether unacquainted. But who would not endure bodily sickness, that the soul may become sound, and every whit whole? Each pang of death will set sin a step nearer the door; and with the last breath, the body of sin will breathe out its last. The pains of death will not last long; and the Lord your God will not leave, but support you under them.

Case 7: *But I am likely to be cut off in the midst of my days.*

Answer: Do not complain; you will be the sooner at home—you thereby have the advantage of your fellow laborers, who were at work before you in the vineyard. God, in the course of his providence, hides some of his saints early in the grave, that they may be taken away from the evil to come. An early removal out of this world, prevents much sin and misery. They have no ground of complaint, who get the residue of their years in Immanuel's land. Surely you shall live as long as you have work cut out for you by the great Master, to be done for him in this world—and when that is at an end, it is high time to be gone.

Case 8: *I am afraid of sudden death.*

Answer: You may indeed die so. Good Eli died suddenly (1 Sam. 4:18). Yet death found him watching (v. 13). "Watch, therefore, for ye know not what hour the Lord doth come" (Matt. 24:42). But be not afraid, it is an inexpressible comfort, that death, come when it will, can never catch you out of Christ; and therefore can never seize you, as a jailor, to hurry you into the prison of hell. Sudden death may hasten and facilitate your passage to heaven, but can do you no prejudice.

Case 9: *I am afraid it will be my lot to die lacking the exercise of reason.*

Answer: I make no question but a child of God, a true Christian, may die in this case. But what harm? There is no hazard in it, as to his eternal state—a disease at death may divest him of his reason, but not of his religion. When a man, going on a long voyage, has put his affairs in order, and put all his goods aboard, he himself may be carried on board the ship sleeping—all is safe with him, although he knows not where he is, until he awakes in the ship. Even so the godly man, who dies in this case, may die uncomfortably, but not unsafely.

Case 10: *I am naturally timorous, and the very thoughts of death are terrible to me.*

Answer: The less you think on death, the thoughts of it will be the more frightful—make it familiar to you by frequent meditations upon it, and you may thereby quiet your fears. Look at the white and bright side of the cloud—take faith's view of the city that has foundations; so shall you see hope in your death. Be duly affected with the body of sin and death, the frequent interruptions of your communion with God, and with the glory which dwells on the other side of death—this will contribute much to remove slavish fear.

It is a pity that saints should be so fond of life as they often are—they ought to be always on good terms with death.

I conclude with a few directions on how to prepare for death, so that we may die comfortably. First, let it be your constant care to keep a clean conscience, "A conscience void to offense toward God, and toward man" (Acts 24:16 KJV). Beware of a standing controversy between God and you, on the account of some iniquity regarded in the heart. When an honest man is about to leave his country, and not to return, he settles accounts with those he had dealings with, and lays down methods for paying his debts in due time, lest he be reckoned a bankrupt, and arrested by an officer when he is going off. Guilt lying on the conscience is a fountain of fears, and will readily sting severely, when death stares the criminal in the face. Hence it is that many, even of God's children, when dying, wish passionately, and desire eagerly, that they may live to do what they ought to have done before that time.

Therefore, walk closely with God; be diligent, strict, and exact in your course—beware of loose, careless, and irregular conversation, as you would not lay up for yourselves anguish and bitterness of spirit in a dying hour. And because, through the infirmity cleaving to us, in our present state of imperfection, in many things we offend all, renew your repentance daily, and be ever washing in the Redeemer's blood. As long as you are in the world, you will need to wash your feet (John 13:10), that is, to make application of the blood of Christ anew, for purging your consciences from the guilt of daily miscarriages. Let death find you at the "fountain"; and, if so, it will find you ready to answer at its call.

Second, be always watchful, waiting for your change, "like unto men that wait for their lord . . . that when he comes and knocks, they may open unto him immediately" (Luke 12:36). Beware of slumbering and sleeping, while the bridegroom tarries. To be awakened out of spiritual slumber, by a surprising call to pass into another world, is a very frightful thing—but he who is daily waiting for the coming of his Lord, will comfortably receive the "grim messenger," while he beholds him ushering in him, of whom he may confidently say, "This is my God, and I have waited for him."

The way to die comfortably is to die daily! Be often essaying, as it were, to die. Bring yourselves familiarly acquainted with death, by making many visits to the grave, in serious meditations upon it. This was Job's practice (17:13–14): "I have made my bed in the darkness."

CS Lewis "Die before you die. After that it is too late."

Go and do likewise; and when death comes, you shall have nothing to do but to lie down. "I have said to corruption, You are my father: to the worm, You are my mother and my sister." You say so too; and you will be the fitter to go home to their house.

Be frequently reflecting upon your conduct, and considering what course of life you wish to be found in, when death arrests you; and act accordingly. When you do the duties of your station in life, or are employed in acts of worship, think with yourselves, that, it may be, this is the last opportunity; and therefore do it as if you were never to do more of that kind. When you lie down at night, compose your spirits, as if you were not to awake until the heavens be no more. And when you awake in the morning, consider that new day as your last; and live accordingly. Surely that night comes, of which you will never see the morning; or that morning, of which you will never see the night. But which of your mornings or nights will be such, you know not.

We are ready for heaven when our heart
is there before us.

Third, employ yourselves much in weaning your hearts from the world. The man who is making ready to go abroad, busies himself in taking leave of his friends. Let the mantel of earthly enjoyments hang loose about you, that it may be easily dropped, when death comes to carry you away into another world. Moderate your affections toward your lawful comforts of life—let not your hearts be too much taken with them. The traveler acts unwisely, who allows himself to be so allured with the "conveniences of the inn" where he lodges, as to make his necessary departure from it grievous. Feed with fear, and walk through the world as pilgrims and strangers. Just as, when the corn is forsaking the ground, it is ready for the sickle; when the fruit is ripe, it falls off the tree easily; so, when a Christian's heart is truly weaned from the world, he is prepared for death, and it will be the more easy to him. A heart disengaged from the world is a heavenly one—we are ready for heaven when our heart is there before us.

Adapted from the chapter, "Death" in *Human Nature in Its Fourfold State* by Thomas Boston.

Thomas Boston (1676–1732) was a Scottish church leader.

Scripture quotations marked KJV are from the *King James Version* of the Bible.

Part Four

A FUTURE
THAT WILL NOT
DISAPPOINT

17

Suffering Hurries the Heart toward Heaven

JONI EARECKSON TADA

There is a connection between hardship and heaven. Samuel Rutherford described it this way in his *Letters*:

> If God had told me some time ago that He was about to make me as happy as I could be in this world, and then had told me that He should begin by crippling me in arm or limb, and removing me from all my usual sources of enjoyment, I should have thought it a very strange mode of accomplishing His purpose. And yet, how is His wisdom manifest even in this! For if you should see a man shut up in a closed room, idolizing a set of lamps and rejoicing in their light, and you wished to make him truly happy, you would begin by blowing out all his lamps; and then throw open the shutters to let in the light of heaven.

That's exactly what God did for me when he sent a broken neck my way. He blew out the lamps in my life that lit up the here and now and made it so captivating. The dark despair of total and permanent paralysis that followed wasn't much fun, but it sure made heaven come alive.

Suffering makes us want to go to heaven. Broken homes and broken hearts crush our illusions that earth can keep its promises; that it can really satisfy. Only the hope of heaven can truly move our passions off the world—which God knows could never fulfill us any-way—and place them where they will find their glorious fulfillment.

When I was on my feet, it would have been nice had I focused on heaven purely for Christ's sake, but forget that. Altruistic, yes. But realistic? No. I was healthy, athletic, distracted, and not the type to get hyped about heaven for anyone's sake other than my own. Who wants to think about heaven when you've got things to do and places to go here? Besides, you have to die in order to get there. I did not want to think about that at the age of seventeen.

It's the nature of the human beast. At least this beast. Some people have to break their necks in order to get their hearts on heavenly glories above, and I happen to be one of them. It was only after the permanency of my paralysis sank in, that heaven interested me.

Thank heaven you don't have to break your neck to get grabbed. When you come to *know* that the hopes you have cherished will never come true, that your loved one is gone from this life forever, that you will never be as pretty or successful or famous as you had once imagined, your sights are lifted. You long and look forward to the day when your hopes will be fulfilled and heartache will vanish. The glorious day when "we will be whole" becomes your passion as you realize that, once and for all, earth can never meet your deepest longings.

My hope of running through earthly meadows and splashing my feet in a stream will never come true—but it will in the new heavens and new earth. My dream of hugging a loved one and actually feeling his or her embrace will never come true—but it will when we stand together before Jesus.

You can appreciate this, especially if earth has broken your heart. You may be a mother who has lost her child in an accident, a son who has lost his father to cancer, or a husband whose wife has passed on to glory. These dear ones take with them a part of your heart that no one can replace. And since the pursuit of heaven is an occupation of the heart anyway, don't be surprised if you find yourself longing for heaven after you leave the graveside. If your heart is with your loved ones, and they are home with the Lord, then heaven is home for you, too.

A broken heart leads to the true contentment of asking less of this life because more is coming in the next. The art of living with suffering is the art of readjusting your expectations in the here and now. There are simply some things I will *never have* because of this wheelchair. Such longings heighten my loneliness here on earth. The psalmist wrapped words around this loneliness in Psalm 73:25–26 when he said, "Whom have I in heaven but You? And besides You, I desire nothing on earth. My flesh and my heart may fail, but God is the strength of my heart and my portion forever."

> A broken heart leads to the true contentment
> of asking less of this life because
> more is coming in the next.

But asking less is not a loss, and readjusting expectations is not a negative. It's good. When I was on my feet, big boisterous pleasures provided only fleeting satisfaction. In a wheelchair, satisfaction settles in as I sit under an oak tree on a windy day and delight in the rustle of leaves or sit by a fire and enjoy the soothing strains of a symphony. These smaller, less noisy pleasures are rich because, unlike the fun on my feet, these things yield patience, endurance, and a spirit of gratitude, all of which fits me further for eternity.

It is this yieldedness that gains you the most here on earth. You enjoy "a sincere heart in full assurance of faith" as it says in Hebrews

10:22, which in turn gives conviction to unseen divine realities and future divine fulfillments. You enjoy a new degree, a new release of energy at every point in your life as the eye of your soul is strengthened and spiritual understanding is quickened. A greater assurance of faith shows you that all things are, indeed, working together for good, and you realize without a doubt that the smallest of kind deeds done in Christ's name will result in a greater capacity to serve God in glory.

Suffering hurries the heart homeward.

Excerpted from *Heaven . . . Your Real Home* by Joni Eareckson Tada. ©1995 by Joni Eareckson Tada. Used by permission of Zondervan.

Joni Eareckson Tada is CEO of Joni and Friends, an organization accelerating Christian ministry in the disability community.

Scripture references are from *The New American Standard Bible*.

18

To Despise This Present Life

JOHN CALVIN

Whatever be the kind of tribulation with which we are afflicted, we should always consider the end of it to be, that we may be trained to despise the present, and thereby stimulated to aspire to the future life. For since God well knows how strongly we are inclined by nature to a slavish love of this world, in order to prevent us from clinging too strongly to it, he employs the fittest reason for calling us back, and shaking off our lethargy.

Every one of us, indeed, would be thought to aspire and aim at heavenly immortality during the whole course of his life. For we would be ashamed in no respect to excel the lower animals; whose condition would not be at all inferior to ours, had we not a hope of immortality beyond the grave. But when you attend to the plans, wishes, and actions of each, you see nothing in them but the earth. Hence our stupidity; our minds being dazzled with the glare of wealth, power, and honors, that they can see no farther. The heart also, engrossed with avarice, ambition, and lust, is weighed down and cannot rise above them. In short, the whole soul, ensnared by the allurements of the flesh, seeks its happiness on the earth.

To meet this disease, the Lord makes his people sensible of the vanity of the present life, by a constant proof of its miseries. Thus, that they may not promise themselves deep and lasting peace in it, he often allows them to be assailed by war, tumult, or rapine, or to be disturbed by other injuries. That they may not long with too much eagerness after fleeting and fading riches, or rest in those which they already possess, he reduces them to want, or, at least, restricts them to a moderate allowance, at one time by exile, at another by sterility, at another by fire, or by other means. That they may not indulge too complacently in the advantages of married life, he either vexes them by the misconduct of their partners, or humbles them by the wickedness of their children, or afflicts them by bereavement.

But if in all these he is indulgent to them, lest they should either swell with vain-glory, or be elated with confidence, by diseases and dangers he sets palpably before them how unstable and evanescent are all the advantages competent to mortals. We duly profit by the discipline of the cross, when we learn that this life, estimated in itself, is restless, troubled, in numberless ways wretched, and plainly in no respect happy; that what are estimated its blessings are uncertain, fleeting, vain, and vitiated by a great admixture of evil. From this we conclude, that all we have to seek or hope for here is contest; that when we think of the crown we must raise our eyes to heaven. For we must hold that our mind never rises seriously to desire and aspire after the future until it has learned to despise the present life.

Our mind never rises seriously to desire
and aspire after the future until it has learned
to despise the present life.

For there is no medium between the two things: the earth must either be worthless in our estimation, or keep us enslaved by an intemperate love of it. Therefore, if we have any regard to eternity, we must carefully strive to disencumber ourselves of these fetters. Moreover, since the present life has many enticements to allure us, and great semblance of delight, grace, and sweetness to soothe us, it is of great consequence to us to be now and then called off from its fascinations. For what, pray, would happen, if we here enjoyed an uninterrupted course of honor and felicity, when even the constant stimulus of affliction cannot arouse us to a due sense of our misery?

In proportion as this improper love diminishes, our desire of a better life should increase. I confess, indeed, that a most accurate opinion was formed by those who thought that the best thing was not to be born, the next best to die early. For, being destitute of the light of God and of true religion, what could they see in it that was not of dire and evil omen? Nor was it unreasonable for those who felt sorrow and shed tears at the birth of their kindred, to keep holiday at their deaths. But this they did without profit; because, devoid of the true doctrine of faith, they saw not how that which in itself is neither happy nor desirable turns to the advantage of the righteous, and hence their opinion issued in despair. Let believers, then, in forming an estimate of this mortal life, and perceiving that in itself it is nothing but misery, make it their aim to exert themselves with greater alacrity, and less hindrance, in aspiring to the future and eternal life. When we contrast the two, the former may not only be securely neglected, but, in comparison of the latter, be disdained and contemned. If heaven is our country, what can the earth be but a place of exile? If departure from the world is entrance into life, what is the world but a sepulcher, and what is residence in it but immersion in death? If to be freed from the body is to gain full possession of freedom, what is the body but a prison? If it is the very summit of happiness to enjoy the presence of God, is it not miserable to want it? But "whilst we are at home in the body, we are absent from the Lord" (2 Cor. 5:6 KJV). Thus when the earthly is compared with the heavenly life, it may undoubtedly be despised and trampled under foot. We ought never, indeed, to regard it with hatred, except in so far as it keeps us subject to sin; and even this hatred ought not to be directed against life itself. At all events, we must stand so affected towards it in regard to weariness or hatred as, while longing for its termination, to be ready at the Lord's will to continue in it, keeping far from everything like murmuring and impatience. For it is as if the Lord had assigned us a post, which we must maintain till he recalls us. Paul, indeed, laments his condition, in being still bound with the fetters of the body, and sighs earnestly for redemption (Rom. 7:24); nevertheless, he declared that, in obedience to the command of God he was prepared for both courses, because he acknowledges it as his duty to God to glorify his name whether by life or by death, while it belongs to God to determine what is most conducive to his glory (Phil. 1:20–24). Wherefore, if it becomes us to live and die to the Lord, let us leave the period of our life and death at his disposal. Still let us ardently long for death, and constantly meditate upon it, and in comparison with future immortality, let us despise life, and, on account of the bondage of sin, long to renounce it whenever it shall so please the Lord.

But, most strange to say, many who boast of being Christians, instead of thus longing for death, are so afraid of it that they tremble at the very mention of it as a thing ominous and dreadful. We cannot wonder, indeed, that our natural feelings should be somewhat shocked at the mention of our dissolution. But it is altogether intolerable that the light of piety should not be so powerful in a Christian breast as with greater consolation to overcome and suppress that fear. For if we reflect that this our tabernacle, unstable, defective, corruptible, fading, pining, and putrid, is dissolved, in order that it may forthwith be renewed in sure, perfect, incorruptible, in fine, in heavenly glory, will not faith compel us eagerly to desire what nature dreads? If we reflect that by death we are recalled from exile to inhabit our native country, a heavenly country, shall this give us no comfort? But everything longs for permanent existence. I admit this, and therefore contend that we ought to look to future immortality, where we may obtain that fixed condition which nowhere appears on the earth. For Paul admirably enjoins believers to hasten cheerfully to death, not because they "would be unclothed, but clothed upon" (2 Cor. 5:4). Shall the lower animals, and inanimate creatures themselves even wood and stone, as conscious of their present vanity, long for the final resurrection, that they may with the sons of God be delivered from vanity (Rom. 8:19); and shall we, endued with the light of intellect, and more than intellect, enlightened by the Spirit of God, when our essence is in question, rise no higher than the corruption of this earth?

No man has made much progress in the school of Christ who does not look forward with joy to the day of death and final resurrection (2 Tim. 4:18; Titus 2:13) for Paul distinguishes all believers by this mark; and the usual course of Scripture is to direct us there whenever it would furnish us with an argument for substantial joy. "Look up," says our Lord, "and lift up your heads; for your redemption draweth nigh" (Luke 21:28). Is it reasonable, I ask, that what he intended to have a powerful effect in stirring us up to alacrity and exultation should produce nothing but sadness and consternation? If it is so, why do we still glory in him as our Master? Therefore, let us come to a sounder mind, and how repugnant so ever the blind and stupid longing of the flesh may be, let us doubt not to desire the advent of the Lord not in wish only, but with earnest sighs, as the most propitious of all events. He will come as a Redeemer to

129

<u>deliver us from an immense abyss of evil and misery, and lead us to
the blessed inheritance of his life and glory</u>.

Excerpted from *The Institutes of the Christian Religion* by John Calvin, Book Third,
chapter 9: "Of Meditating on the Future Life."

John Calvin (1509–1564) was an influential French theologian and pastor during
the Protestant Reformation.

19

The Day of a Godly Man's Death

JONATHAN EDWARDS

"A good name is better than precious ointment; and the day of death than the day of one's birth" (Eccles. 7:1). The day of a godly man's death is better than the day of his birth. This is as contrary as possible to the notions commonly entertained by men who look on the day of a man's birth as a happy day but the day of death as the most sorrowful and doleful day that man ever met with.

There is nothing that man has so great a dread of and such terrible apprehension of as death. 'Tis generally looked upon as the end of all good to a man, as entrance in a doleful state of oblivion and darkness and eternal separation from all enjoyment.

But when a godly man dies, he receives a better life than when he is born. We call it death. It signifies the end of life or the abolishing and destruction of it, and it is so in appearance. But it is in reality the beginning of a more glorious life. Therefore, God, who sees things as they are, doesn't call a godly man's decease by the name of death, but in the Scriptures calls it sleep. Thus it is said of Stephen who was stoned to death in Acts 7:60, "When he had said this, he fell asleep." So 1 Corinthians 15:18 says, "They also which are fallen asleep in Christ."

And Christ, not accounting the decease of a godly man worthy of the name of death, says that he who believes in him shall not die.

John 6:49–50 says, "Your fathers did eat manna in the wilderness, and are dead. This is the bread which cometh down from heaven, that a man may eat thereof, and not die." And John 6:51 says, "If any man eat of this bread, he shall live for ever." A godly man's death is indeed more like a resurrection or a rising from the dead than like death. The present life is but a state of death in comparison of that glorious life that a godly man enters into when he dies. He enters into the more glorious and blessed state. He does, as it were, awake out of sleep and therefore this change is implied in Psalm 17:15, "I shall be satisfied, when I awake."

> The present life is but a state of death
> in comparison of that glorious life that a
> godly man enters into when he dies.

In the day of a man's birth, he receives the bodily and natural life. The present life is a state wherein the godly are exceeding clogged with the flesh and with sin. They are in a great measure hammered and deadened and rendered insensible and inactive in comparison of what they are in another world. But when a godly man dies, he receives the life of angels. He is made a partaker of the glorious life of Jesus Christ. When a man is born, he receives a short, fading, and uncertain life, but when a godly man dies, he receives eternal life. When a man is born, he then becomes mortal; but when he dies, he receives an immortal life. The life that a person receives on the day of his birth is not worthy to be called by the name of life in comparison of that which the godly receive at the day of their death. The godly who are dead now live. They live now indeed and never lived before with that which is worthy to be called with the name of life.

The godly person receives spiritual life before in his conversion, but on the day of his death, he receives the life of glory. They have a life now that is more perfect, happy, and glorious—ten thousand times—than the best and happiest life on earth. The image of God is completed, and all sin wholly and perfectly abolished. Sin is a kind of death that cleaves to the soul. The remains of that in a godly man are reminders of death. But when a godly man departs this life, he is delivered from all remains of death. He is then delivered from the body of his death. Holiness, which is life that is given him but as a spark, shall be a flame then and shall make the soul to shine forth as the sun in the kingdom of God.

A godly person on the day of his death enters into a better world than on the day of his birth. 'Tis on the day of one's birth that one first comes into the world, comes abroad from being shut up in the womb into the world. But the soul of a godly man on the day of his death enters upon a state of more glorious liberty. It is like one escaped from prison. His soul is released from the body where it was confined and kept in prison under the chains of sin and the flesh. It escapes from this world that is a loathsome dungeon in comparison to that more glorious world that it enters into. The day of a godly man's death is the day wherein his soul is born into that glorious world.

The world that a man comes into on the day of his birth is a world of low and earthly enjoyment. But the world that the soul of a godly man is born into on the day of his death is a world of spiritual and divine enjoyments. This is a world of fading, vanishing pleasures, but that is a world of substantial, durable joys and delights. There are pleasures forevermore.

This world that men come into on the day of their birth is a world of sin and vanity and trouble. But the world that a godly man enters into on the day of his death is a world of perfection and holiness, of light and joy without any mixture of sin and sorrow. This earth is a valley of tears, but that is Mount Zion, where they sing a new and everlasting song. Where all tears are wiped from their eyes, and "sorrow and sighing shall flee away" (Isa. 35:10), where there is "no more death, neither sorrow, nor crying, neither shall there be any more pain: for the former things are passed away" (Rev. 21:4).

When a godly man dies, he enters into a world that has better inhabitants, and where there is better company than the world that he entered into on the day of his birth. This world that persons enter into on the day of their birth is a world that is full of wicked men, those whose hearts are full of hateful lusts and vile and unlovely dispositions, whereby they make one another miserable. But a godly man, on the day of his death, goes into a world where the inhabitants are all righteous and have no lusts in their hearts. They are all most excellent and lovely and full of love as what reigns in their hearts. They are united in the dearest friendship and with whom the departed saints converse in the most pleasant manner, without any to spoil or mar their conversation.

On the day of a person's birth, he is born into a world that is under a curse and has no guard against it; but on the day of his death, he enters into a world that is blessed of God, where there is no more curse, but only joy and happiness, a world that is blessed continually with the glorious presence of God and the perfect manifestation and full enjoyment of God's love. 'Tis a world that is filled with the boundless love of God which does, as a river of life, satisfy all the inhabitants thereof.

A godly person on the day of his death is brought to behold a more pleasant and glorious light than he did on the day of his birth. 'Tis on the day of a man's birth that he first beholds the light. He comes then to see the light of the sunlight, and it's a thing sweet to men. A man on the day of his death closes his eyes forever on this light. Though he closes his eyes on the light of the sun, he opens them in the midst of the light of God's glory, who is the Father of lights, who hath clothed the sun with light, in comparison of which the light of the sun is a dark shade. He sees the light of the Sun of Righteousness of him who is the brightness of his Father. He sees no more of the light of this lower world, but he is blessed with the light of the heaven of heavens where they have "no need of the sun, neither of the moon" (Rev. 21:23), nor of the light of a candle, "for the Lord God giveth them light" (Rev. 22:5), "and the Lamb is the light thereof" (Rev. 21:23).

The light of the sun discovers many pleasant objects to us. It discovers to us the faces of men, the faces of our friends, and the face of the earth with the trees and fields and many bountiful appearances that are the works of nature. The godly man on the day of his death enters where he may behold an infinitely more glorious one. He may behold God. Matthew 5:8 says, "Blessed are the pure in heart: for they shall see God."

The godly person on the day of his death is received by a better parent than persons are received by on the day of their birth. Persons are joyfully received on the day of their birth by their earthly parents, but death snatches them from them and from all earthly friends. A godly person on the day of his death leaves them in sackcloth and tears but is received into the arms of a heavenly Father. He is welcomed into his immediate and glorious presence and to the full enjoyment of his love to be in heaven forever. He will be in his family to dwell with his children and eat and drink at his table with them. He will partake with Jesus Christ his Son and with the glorified saints and angels, his dear children in the palace of his glory.

But a godly man on the day of his death is more joyfully

welcomed into heaven than he is received by his earthly parents on the day of his birth. Indeed there is oftentimes a great weeping among earthly friends on the day of a godly man's death, but there is joy among his heavenly friends when they meet him and welcome him to Mount Zion, the city of the living God.

The pious soul on the day of his death is received to a better inheritance than on the day of his birth. A person on the day of his birth may be heir to a great estate. He may on the day of his birth come to be an heir of large earthly possessions. Death takes persons away from all their earthly possessions. If they have been in comfortable circumstances, or if they have been rich, death takes them away from all, but it translates them into better possessions, a more glorious inheritance. First Peter 1:4 says, "To an inheritance incorruptible, and undefiled, and that fadeth not away, reserved in heaven for you." They are then received to the possession of a kingdom, a crown of life, and to unspeakable and unsearchable riches and glory.

Thus, the day of a godly man's death is better than the day of his birth on the account of the glorious change made in his circumstances by his death. Even in the midst of the valley of the shadow of death, the godly man has cause to rejoice at the approaches of it, to bid it welcome, so for him to die is gain. And oftentimes God actively gives much of the light of his presence that carries above all the fears of death. God sometimes gives such a sense of his love, such discoveries of being, such views of approaching glory and happiness that make the day of death a pleasant day, more pleasant and more joyful than a wedding day and sometimes the most pleasant day that ever he saw in his life (Ps. 37:3).

I would urge persons to get into such a state that the day of their death may be so to them. Strive that you may be godly persons. That you may have your heart changed and nature savingly renewed.

Then it will be thus with you—that the day of your death will be better than the day of your birth.

Condensed and edited from the Jonathan Edwards sermon "The Day of a Godly Man's Death Is Better Than the Day of His Birth" as published in *The Blessing of God: Previously Unpublished Sermons of Jonathan Edwards* © 2003 by Michael McMullen, editor, published by Broadman & Holman, Nashville, TN. Used by permission.

Jonathan Edwards (1703–1758) was a colonial American Congregational preacher, theologian, missionary to native Americans, and president of the College of New Jersey, which later became Princeton University.

Scripture references are from the *King James Version* of the Bible.

20

Let Us Say in Dying, *"Lord Jesus, Receive My Spirit"*

R. L. DABNEY

It is somewhat remarkable that under each dispensation the first believer's death which is recorded was that of a martyr. In the Old Testament it was that of Abel; in the New that of Stephen. There is a peculiar interest in the death of the first Christian of the new dispensation; for the grave and the world of spirits had now received a new illustration. The saints of the Old Testament had, indeed, good hope that "their souls should not be left in Hades." But the instructions and the resurrection of Christ had now illuminated the tomb with a new flood of light and hope.

> There the dear flesh of Jesus lay,
> And left a long perfume.[1]

His death had now conquered the king of terrors, disarmed him of his sting, and led captivity captive. Believers, with such an example, must surely learn a new lesson of submission and courage. Accordingly, the death of the proto-martyr, although accompanied with every outward circumstance of cruelty and horror, was full of consolation and peace. Persecuted upon the unjust charge of perverting the religion of Moses, he had defended himself and rebuked his accusers' sins with a faithful boldness by which they were cut to the heart, insomuch that they gnashed upon him with their teeth. His justification of himself and his charges against them were unanswerable; but they resolved at once to silence his voice and to gratify their malignity by his death. He was condemned to that ghastly mode of execution, stoning to death with stones. Surrounded with a raging multitude who were rather wild beasts than men, he was dragged out of the city. And while a young Pharisee named Saul, afterwards the great Apostle of the Gentiles, kept the clothes of the executioners, they stoned Stephen, whose dying prayer was, "Lord Jesus, receive my spirit."

This prayer seems to teach us that Stephen regarded Jesus Christ as very God. The heavens had just been opened to him, and the celestial realities had been disclosed, with the position of Jesus at the right hand of the Father. And now, immediately after this vision, and amidst the solemn emotions of the last hour, he prays to Jesus Christ, addressing to him the most momentous petition which the creature can raise to deity: "Lord Jesus, receive my spirit" (Acts 7:59 KJV).

In the hour of death especially, the Christian needs a Savior who is no less than God. An angel could not sympathize with our trial, for they cannot feel the pangs of dissolution. A human friend cannot travel with us the path through the dark valley; for the creature that yields to the stroke of death is overwhelmed, and returns no more to guide his fellow. The God-man alone can sustain us; he has felt the mortal blow, for he is man; he has survived it, and returns triumphing to succor us, for he is God. Unless this divine guide be with us, we must fight the battle with the last enemy alone and unaided.

Just when the struggle becomes most fearful to the soul, the veil of approaching dissolution descending between it and all this world shuts it off in the outer darkness; and then, in vast solitary night, must the king of terrors be met, with no human arm to succor and

140

no ear to hear the cry of despair that is lost in the infinite silence. So must you die, my friend, and I. Though wife and children, and officious comrades be crowding around your bed, and loved ones be stooping to receive your last sigh to their very hearts, and your dying head be pillowed upon the bosom which was the dearest resting place of your sorrows while living, the last approach of death will separate you from them all, and you will meet him alone. The icy shadow of his dart, as it comes near your heart, will obstruct all the avenues of sense by which their sympathy can reach you. Even then, practically, you will die alone; as truly alone as the last wanderer in some vast wilderness, who falls exhausted on the plain, and sees nothing above but the burning sky, or around save the boundless waste; as truly alone as the mariner who, when the ship is rushing before a gale through the midnight sea, drops from the mast-head, and buffets vainly with the innumerable billows amidst the pitchy darkness, while his despairing shriek is drowned by the tumult of the deep.

[Christ] alone of all the universe has
fathomed the deepest abysses of death,
has explored all its caverns of despair,
and has returned from them a conqueror.

But then it is that Jesus Christ draws near as an omnipotent Savior. He alone of all the universe has fathomed the deepest abysses of death, has explored all its caverns of despair, and has returned from them a conqueror. He is not only sympathizing man, but omnipresent God, who can go with us into the penetralia of the court of death. When our last labor comes, then let us say, brethren,

"Lord Jesus, receive my spirit" (Acts 7:59). "Where I pass through the valley of the shadow of death, be thou with me; let thy rod and thy staff comfort me" (Ps. 23:4).

2. Second, I am taught by this prayer of the martyr to expect an immediate entrance into the blessed presence of Jesus Christ. I see here that Stephen believed that "the souls of believers are, at their death, made perfect in holiness, and do immediately pass into glory."[2] He evidently did not expect that the grave would absorb his spirit into a state of unconscious sleep, to last until the final consummation; or that any *limbus*, or purgatory, was to swallow him for a time in its fiery bosom. His faith aspired directly to the arms of Christ, and to that blessed world where his glorified humanity now dwells.

Some would persuade us that death is an unconscious sleep; that the soul is not a distinct substance, possessed of its own being and powers of thought independent of the body, but a mere phenomenon, the result of the body's organic action, as sound is of the vibration of the musical chord; and that so there is an absolute suspension of the soul's conscious existence until such time as the body is reared from the dust in the resurrection. So thought not the inspired martyr. He manifestly regarded his spirit as separable from the body, and therefore as a true, independent substance. The latter he relinquishes to the insults of his enemies; the former he commits to Jesus Christ. So taught not that Savior and his two favored disciples when they showed us Moses and Elijah in glory. So promised not the dying Redeemer to the penitent thief, when he said, "This day thou shalt be with me in paradise" (Luke 23:43). His body was left upon the tree a prey to the brutality of his executioners, and probably to ravenous birds. Yet his soul, the true being, passed with his dying Redeemer into immediate blessedness. So believed not Paul when he said that to him to live was Christ, and to die was gain,

(Phil. 1:21), and that to be absent from the body was to be present with the Lord (2 Cor. 5:8).

And would he ever have been in a strait between the two desires, to live and labor for his converts and to die, had the latter been a sleep of dreary ages in the dust? Surely this zealous laborer for Christ could not have hesitated between the choice of such a useless, unconscious blank on the one hand, and a life of praise and of happy activity on earth on the other hand, albeit it was checkered with toils and persecutions. (See Luke 9:30–31; 23:43; Rom. 8:1, 33; 2 Cor. 5:8; Phil. 1:21–23).

3. Third, we learn from the text to what guidance the Christian may commit his soul during its unknown journey into the world of spirits. When death batters down the walls of the earthly tabernacle, to what place shall the dispossessed soul set out? To what direction shall it turn in beginning its mysterious journey? It knows not; it needs a skillful, powerful, and friendly guide.

But more; it is a journey into a spiritual world, and this thought makes it awful to the apprehensions of man. The presence of one dis-embodied spirit in the solitude of night would shake us with a thrill of dread. This journey into the unknown world must, else, issue in our introduction to a scene whose awful novelties will overpower our faculties; for even the very thought of them, when they are permitted to dwell upon our hearts, fills us with a sense of dreadful suspense. Truly will the trembling soul need someone on whom to lean, some mighty, experienced, and tender guardian, who will point the way to the prepared mansions, and cheer and sustain its fainting courage. That guide is Christ—therefore let us say, in dying, "Lord Jesus, receive my spirit" (Acts 7:59).

And when the walls of the flesh are battered away by death, the vision of the spiritual world will flow in upon us unobstructed. Not seldom does the deathbed of Christ's people present instances which seem as though some gleams of that celestial light, and some glimpses of the beings who inhabit it, begin to reach the dying saint before he quite leaves the clay, through the rents which are made in his frail tabernacle by the strokes of the last enemy. What is it that sometimes makes the sunken countenance light up in the article of death with a sudden glory, and the eye, but now devoid of speculation, beam with one more expiring flash of heaven's light? Has the soul seen through the torn veil already the angels' faces bending over its agony, and heard their tender call, unheard by ears of flesh, wooing it out of the crumbling body?

When the martyr uttered the prayer of the text he manifestly looked to the arms of Christ as his final home. We are authorized by his example to say, "Lord Jesus, receive my spirit, not only that you may sustain it in the pangs of dying and guide it to its heavenly home, and clothe it in your own robe of righteousness and answer for it in the great day of accounts, but that it may dwell with you in a world without end. You did pray, 'Father, I desire that they also whom you have given me, may be with me where I am, to see my glory'; and you the Father hears always. You did show the holy Apostle that, after you come with the voice of the archangel and the trumpet of God, we shall ever be with the Lord. You have taught us that, when you shall appear, we shall be like you; for we shall see you as you are."

Oh! Blessed resting place! "In thy presence is fulness of joy; at thy right hand are pleasures for evermore" (Ps. 16:11 KJV). Let us, brethren, live and die like believing Stephen, and our spirits will be received to the place where the God-man holds his regal court, to go out thence no more forever. We shall see him on his throne, so gloriously earned. We shall see the very hands which were pierced for us; not then bleeding, but reaching forth to us the scepter of universal dominion to guide and protect us. We shall hear the very voice which once said, "Come unto me, all who labor and are heavy laden," bidding our souls welcome to his glory. And as we gaze and adore and praise, we shall be changed by his Spirit into the same image of holiness.

Adapted from "Our Comfort in Dying," a sermon by R. L. Dabney.

Robert Lewis Dabney (1820–1898) was a Southern Presbyterian pastor, theologian, and a Confederate Army chaplain.

Scripture quotations marked KJV are from the *King James Version* of the Bible.

21

Those Who Die Daily Die Easily

CHARLES HADDON SPURGEON

It is the general custom with sick people to talk about "getting well"; and those who visit them, even when they are gracious people, will see the tokens of death upon them and yet will speak as if they were hopeful of their recovery. I remember a father asking me when I prayed with a consumptive girl to be sure not to mention death. In such cases it would be far more sensible for the sick man to turn his thoughts towards eternity, and stand prepared for the great change. When our God by our affliction calls upon us to number our days, let us not refuse to do so.

I admire the wisdom of Job, that he does not shirk the subject of death, but dwells upon it as an appropriate topic, saying, "I know that thou wilt bring me to death, and to the house appointed for all living" (Job 30:23). Yet Job made a mistake in the hasty conclusion which he drew from his grievous affliction. Under depression of spirit he felt sure that he must very soon die; he feared that God would not relax the blows of his hand until his body became a ruin, and then he would have rest. But he did not die at that time. He was fully recovered, and God gave him twice as much as he had before.

It is the part of a brave man, and especially of a believing man, neither to dread death nor to sigh for it; neither to fear it nor to court it. In patience possessing his soul, he should not despair of life when hardly pressed; and he should be always more eager to run his race well than to reach its end. It is no work of men of faith to predict their own deaths. These things are with God. How long we shall live on earth we know not, and need not wish to know. We have not the choosing of short or long life; and if we had such choice, it would be wise to refer it back to our God. "Father, into thy hands I commend my spirit" (Luke 23:46) is an admirable prayer for living as well as for dying saints. To wish to pry between the folded leaves of the book of destiny is to desire a questionable privilege: doubtless we live the better because we cannot foresee the moment when this life shall reach its finis.

You say that you cannot abide the thought of death. Then you greatly need it. Your shrinking from it proves that you are not in a right state of mind, or else you would take it into due consideration without reluctance. That is a poor happiness which overlooks the most important of facts. I would not endure a peace which could only be maintained by thoughtlessness. You have something yet to learn if you are a Christian, and yet are not prepared to die. You need to reach a higher state of grace, and attain to a firmer and more forceful faith. That you are as yet a babe in grace is clear from your admission that to depart and be with Christ does not seem to be a better thing for you than to abide in the flesh.

Should it not be the business of this life to prepare for the next life, and, in that respect, to prepare to die? But how can a man be prepared for that which he never thinks of? Do you mean to take a leap in the dark? If so, you are in an unhappy condition, and I beseech you as you love your own soul to escape from such peril by the help of God's Holy Spirit.

Perhaps Job had not always said, "I know that thou wilt bring me to death" (Job 30:23); but now, as he sits upon the dunghill, and scrapes himself with the potsherd, and writhes in anguish, and is depressed in spirit, he realizes his own mortality. When the tent pole quivers in the storm, and the covering thereof flaps to and fro in the wind, and the whole structure threatens to dissolve in the tempest, then the tenant of the habitation, chilled to his marrow, needs not to be instructed that his tabernacle is frail: he knows it well enough. We need many touches of the rod of affliction before we really learn the undeniable truth of our mortality.

Every man, woman, and child in this place would unite with me in saying, "I know that thou wilt bring *me* to death"; and yet it is highly probable that a large number of us do not know this to be so. "It is a commonplace matter of fact which we all admit," cries one. I know it is so; and yet in the very commonness of the truth there lies a temptation to overlook its personal application. We know this as though we knew it not. To many it is not taken into the reckoning, and it is not a factor in their being. They do not number their days so as to apply their hearts unto wisdom.

That poet was half inspired who said, "All men count all men mortal but themselves." Is it not so with us? We do not really expect to die. We reckon that we shall live a very considerable time yet. Even those who are very aged still think that as a few others have lived to an extreme old age, so may they. I am afraid there are few who could say with a gracious soldier, "I thank God I fear not death. These thirty years together I never rose from my bed in the morning and reckoned upon living till night."

Those who die daily will die easily. Those who make themselves familiar with the tomb will find it transfigured into a bed—the charnel will become a couch. The man who rejoices in the covenant of grace is cheered by the fact that even death itself is comprehended among the things which belong to the believer. I would to God we had learned this lesson. We should not then put death aside among the lumber, nor set it upon the shelf among the things which we never intend to use.

Let us live as dying men among dying men, and then we shall truly live. This will not make us unhappy; for surely no heir of heaven will fret because he is not doomed to live here forever. It would be a sad sentence if we were bound over to dwell in this poor world forever. If the Supreme should say, "Live here forever," it would be a malediction rather than a benediction. To grow ripe and to be carried home like shocks of corn in their season—is not this a fit and fair thing? To labor through a blessed day and then at nightfall to go home and to receive the wages of grace—is there anything dark and dismal about that? God forgive you that you ever thought so! If you are the Lord's own child, I invite you to look this homegoing in the face until you change your thought and see no more in it of gloom and dread, but a very heaven of hope and glory.

To labor through a blessed day and then
at nightfall to go home and to receive
the wages of grace—is there anything dark
and dismal about that?

Job, even in his anguish, does not for a moment forget his God. He speaks of him here: "I know that *thou* wilt bring me to death." *He perceives that he will not die apart from God.* He does not say his sore boils or his strangulation will bring him to death; but "thou wilt bring me to death." He does not trace his approaching death to chance, or to fate, or to second causes; no, he sees only the hand of the Lord. To him belong both life and death. Say not that the wasting consumption took away your darling; complain not that a fierce fever slew your father; but feel that the Lord himself has done it. "It is the LORD: let him do what seemeth him good" (1 Sam. 3:18). Blame not the accident, neither complain of the pestilence; for Jehovah himself gathers home his own. He only will remove you and me. "I know that thou wilt bring me to death." There is to my heart much delicious comfort in the language before us. I love that old-fashioned verse—

> Plagues and deaths around me fly
> Till he bids I cannot die;
> Not a single shaft can hit
> Till the God of Love thinks fit.[1]

In the midst of malaria and pest we are safe with God. "Because thou hast made the LORD, which is my refuge, even the Most High, thy habitation; there shall no evil befall thee, neither shall any plague come nigh thy dwelling" (Ps. 91:9–10). Beneath the shadow of Jehovah's wing we need not be afraid for the terror by night, nor for the arrow that flies by day, nor for the pestilence that walks in darkness. We are immortal till our work is done. Be, therefore, quiet in the day of evil; rest peaceful in the day of destruction—all things are ordered by wisdom, and precious in the sight of the Lord is the death of his saints. No forces yet in the world are outside of his control. God suffers no foes to trespass on the domain of Providence. All things are ordained of God, and specially are our deaths under the peculiar oversight of our exalted Lord and Savior. He lives and was dead, and bears the keys of death at his girdle. He himself shall guide us through death's iron gate. Surely what the Lord wills and what he himself works cannot be otherwise than acceptable to his chosen! Let us rejoice that in life and in death we are in the Lord's hands.

The text seems to me to cover another sweet and comforting

thought, namely, that *God will be with us in death.* "I know that thou wilt bring me to death." He will bring us on our journey till he brings us to the journey's end—himself our convoy and our leader. We shall have the Lord's company even to our dying hour: "Thou wilt bring me to death." He leads me even to those still waters which men so much fear. "Yea, though I walk through the valley of the shadow of death, I will fear no evil: for thou art with me; thy rod and thy staff they comfort me" (Ps. 23:4). Beloved, we live with God, do we not? Shall we not die with him?

Our life is one long holiday when the Lord Jesus keeps us company—will he leave us at the end? Because God is with us we go forth with joy, and are led forth with peace; the mountains and the hills break forth before us into singing, and all the trees of the field do clap their hands. Will they not be equally glad when we rise to our eternal reward? It is not living that is happiness, but living with God; it is not dying that will be wretchedness, but dying without God. The child has to go to bed, but it does not cry if mother is going upstairs with it. It is quite dark; but what of that? The mother's eyes are lamps to the child. It is very lonely and still. Not so; the mother's arms are the child's company, and her voice is its music. O Lord, when the hour comes for me to go to bed, I know that you will take me there, and speak lovingly into my ear; therefore I cannot fear, but will even look forward to that hour of your manifested love. You had not thought of that, had you? You have been afraid of death—but you cannot be so any longer if your Lord will bring you there in his arms of love. Dismiss all fear, and calmly proceed on your way, though the shades thicken around you; for the Lord is your light and your salvation.

This should be our ordinary condition in daily life; and it is an admirable preparation for thinking of death with composure. Let me live, if God will be with me in life; let me die, if he will be with me in death. So long as we are "forever with the Lord," what matters where else we are? We will not further ask when or where—our *when* is "forever," our where is "with the Lord." Delight in God is the cure for dread of death.

Adapted from the sermon "Concerning Death" by C. H. Spurgeon, delivered on September 26, 1886.

Charles Haddon Spurgeon (1834–1892) was a British Reformed Baptist preacher who is still known as the "Prince of Preachers."

Scripture references are from the *King James Version* of the Bible.

22

God Reserves the Best for the Last

RICHARD SIBBES

Death is ours and for our good. It does us more good than all the friends we have in the world. It determines and ends all our misery and sin; and it is the suburbs of heaven. It lets us into those joys above.

But may not a good Christian fear death? No, so far as a Christian is led with the Spirit of God, and is truly spiritual; for the Spirit carries us upward. But as far as we are earthly and carnal, and biased downward to things below, we are loathe to depart from here.

In some cases God's children are afraid to die, because their accounts are not ready. Though they love Christ, and are in a good way, yet they have not prepared themselves. As a woman that has her husband abroad and desires his coming, but all is not prepared in the house, therefore she desires that he may stay awhile. But as far as we are guided by the Spirit of God sanctifying us, and are in such a condition as we should be in, so far the thoughts of death ought not to be terrible to us; nor indeed are they.

Beloved, there is none but a Christian that can desire death; because it is the end of all comfort here, it is the end of all callings and employments, of all sweetness whatsoever in this world. If another man that is not a Christian, desire heaven, he desires it not as heaven, or to be with Christ as Christ; he desires it under some notion suitable to his corruption; for our desires are as ourselves are, as our aims are. A worldly man cannot go beyond the world. It is his sphere. A carnal man cannot go beyond the flesh. Therefore a carnal man cannot desire heaven. A man that is under the power of any lust can desire nothing but the satisfying of that lust. Heaven is no place for such.

None but a child of God can desire that; for if we consider heaven, and to be with Christ, to be perfect holiness, can he desire it that hates holiness here? Can he desire the image of God upon him that hates it in others and in himself, too? Can he desire the communion of saints, that of all societies hates it the most? Can he desire to be free from sin, that engulfs himself continually in sin? He cannot.

God reserves the best for the last. God's last works are his best works. The new heaven and the new earth are the best; the second wine that Christ created himself was the best; spiritual things are better than natural. A Christian's last is his best.

God will have it so, for the comfort of Christians, that every day they live, they may think, my best is not yet, my best is to come. That every day they rise, they may think, I am nearer heaven one day than I was before, I am nearer death, and therefore nearer to Christ. What a solace is this to a gracious heart! A Christian is a happy man in his life, but happier in his death, because then he goes to Christ; but happiest of all in heaven, for then he is *with Christ.*

A Christian is a happy man in his life,
but happier in his death,
because then he goes to Christ.

But how shall we attain this sanctified sweet desire that Paul had, to die, and be with Christ? *Let us carry ourselves as Paul did,* and then we shall have the same desires. Saint Paul before death, in his lifetime, had his "conversation . . . in heaven" (Phil 3:20 KJV). His mind was there, and his soul followed after. There is no man's soul that comes into heaven, but his mind is there first. It was an easy matter for him to desire to be with Christ, having his conversation in heaven already. Paul in meditation was where he was not, and he was not where he was. He was in heaven when his body was on earth.

Saint Paul had loosed his affections from all earthly things; therefore it was an easy matter for him to desire to be with Christ. "I am crucified to the world, and the world is crucified to me" (Gal. 6:14). If once a Christian comes to this pass, death will be welcome to him. Those whose hearts are fastened to the world cannot easily desire Christ.

Saint Paul labored to keep a good conscience in all things. "Herein I exercise myself, to have a good conscience towards God and men" (Acts 24:16). A guilty conscience trembles at the mention of death. Oh, beloved, the exercising of the heart to keep a clear conscience can only breed this desire in us to depart and to be with Christ.

Paul had assurance that he was in Christ, by his union with him. "I live not," Paul said, "but Christ lives in me" (Gal. 2:20). Therefore labor for assurance of salvation, that you may feel the Spirit of Christ in you, sanctifying and altering your carnal dispositions to be like his. If we would come to Paul's desire, labor to come to the frame of the holy Apostle's spirit. He knew whom he had believed; he was assured that nothing could separate him from the love of God, neither life, nor death, nor anything whatsoever that could befall him (Rom. 8:38–39).

Paul had an art of sweetening the thoughts of death. He considered it only as a departure from earth to heaven. When death was presented unto him as a passage to Christ, it was an easy matter to desire the same; therefore, it should be the art of Christians to present death as a passage to a better life, to labor to bring our souls into such a condition, as to think death not to be a death to us, but the death of itself. Death dies when I die, and I begin to live when I die. It is a sweet passage to life. We never live till we die. This was Paul's art. He had a care to look beyond death, to heaven; and when he looked upon death, he looked on it but as a passage to Christ; so let it be our art and skill. Would we cherish a desire to die—let us look on death as a passage to Christ, and look beyond it to heaven. All of us must go through this dark passage to Christ, which when we consider as Paul did, it will be an easy matter to die.

Therefore, if we desire to end our days in joy and comfort, let us now lay the foundation of a comfortable death. To die well is not a thing of that light moment as some imagine: it is no easy matter. But to die well is a matter of every day. Let us daily do some good that may help us at the time of our death. Every day by repentance pull out the sting of some sin, that so when death comes, we may have nothing to do but to die.

To die well is the action of the whole life. He never dies well for the most part that dies not daily, as Paul said of himself, "I die daily" (1 Cor. 15:31 KJV); he labored to loose his heart from the world, and worldly things. If we loose our hearts from the world and die daily, how easy will it be to die at last! He that thinks of the vanity of the world, and of death, and of being with Christ forever, and is dying daily, it will be easy for him to end his days with comfort.

Adapted from Richard Sibbes sermon "Christ Is Best, or, St. Paul's Strait."

Richard Sibbes (1577–1635) was an English Puritan theologian.

Scripture quotations marked KJV are from the *King James Version* of the Bible.

Give me to know that heaven is all love,
where the eye affects the heart,
and the continual viewing of thy beauty keeps
the soul in continual transports of delight.

Give me to know that heaven is all peace,
where error, pride, rebellion, passion raise no head.

Give me to know that heaven is all joy,
the end of believing, fasting, praying, mourning,
humbling, watching, fearing, repining;

And lead me to it soon.

THE VALLEY OF VISION

Notes

Preface

1. From Joseph Bayly's Out of Mind column in *Eternity* magazine, in a piece titled "Three Sons," published in 1966.

Chapter 3: He Called Death Sweet Names

1. Archibald Alexander, *Thoughts on Religious Experience* (London: The Banner of Truth Trust, 1967), 207.

Chapter 5: Is Christ Our Sickness-Bearer?

1. A. J. Gordon, *The Ministry of Healing, or Miracles of Cure in all Ages*, ©1895 American Baptist Publication Society, Philadelphia, PA.

Chapter 20: Let Us Say in Dying, "Lord Jesus, Receive My Spirit"

1. Isaac Watts, "Why Do We Mourn Departing Friends?" in *Hymns and Spiritual Songs*, 1707.

2. Westminster Shorter Catechism, Question 37, http://www.westminstershorter catechism.net.

Chapter 21: Those Who Die Daily Die Easily

1. John Ryland, "Decrees of God," 1777.